PRESENTING

Paula Danziger

Twayne's United States Authors Series
Young Adult Authors

Patricia J. Campbell, General Editor

TUSAS 651

Paula Danziger

PRESENTING
Paula Danziger

Kathleen Krull

Twayne Publishers
An Imprint of Simon & Schuster Macmillan
New York

Prentice Hall International
London Mexico City New Delhi Singapore Sydney Toronto

Twayne United States Authors Series No. 651

Presenting Paula Danziger
Kathleen Krull

Twayne Publishers
An Imprint of Simon & Schuster Macmillan
866 Third Avenue
New York, NY 10022

The news report by NPR's Vera Frankl was originally broadcast on National Public
Radio's "All Things Considered" on January 16, 1993, and is used with the permission
of National Public Radio. Any unauthorized duplication is strictly prohibited.
Interview © Copyright National Public Radio ® 1993.

Twayne gratefully acknowledges the publishers and individuals who permitted the use
of the following illustrations in copyright:

In the photo insert: pp. 1–11, illustrations kindly provided by Paula Danziger; p. 12,
illustration by Tony Ross reprinted by permission of G. P. Putnam's Sons from
AMBER BROWN IS NOT A CRAYON by Paula Danziger, illustrations copyright
© 1994 by Tony Ross, and by permission of William Heinemann Ltd.; pp. 13–16,
PAULA LIFESTYLE MAGAZINE reprinted by permission of Heinemann Young
Books, photographs copyright © Katie Vandyck 1993.

Library of Congress Cataloging-in-Publication Data

Krull, Kathleen.
    Presenting Paula Danziger / Kathleen Krull.
        p.   cm. — (Twayne's United States authors series ; TUSAS 651)
    Includes bibliographical references and index.
    ISBN 0-8057-4153-4
    1. Danziger, Paula, 1944–   —Criticism and interpretation.
  2. Young adult fiction, American—History and criticism.
  [1. Danziger, Paula, 1944– —Criticism and interpretation.
  2. American literature—History and criticism.] I. Title.
  II. Series.
  PS3554.A585Z74   1995
  813'.54—dc20
                                       94–42014
                                          CIP
                                          AC

CURR
PS
3554
A585
274
1995

to my mother

Contents

Foreword

The advent of Twayne's Young Adult Author Series in 1985 was a response to the growing stature and value of adolescent literature and the lack of serious critical evaluation of the new genre. The first volume of the series was heralded as marking the coming-of-age of young adult fiction.

The aim of the series is twofold. First, it enables young readers to research the work of their favorite authors, and to see them as real people. Each volume is written in a lively, readable style and attempts to present in an attractive, accessible format a vivid portrait of the author as a person.

Second, the series provides teachers and librarians with insights and background material for promoting and teaching young adult novels. Each of the biocritical studies is a serious literary analysis of one author's work (or one sub-genre within young adult literature), with attention to plot structure, theme, character, setting, and imagery. In addition, many of the series writers delve deeper into the creative writing process by tracking down early drafts or unpublished manuscripts by their subject authors, consulting with their editors or other mentors, and examining influences from literature, film, or social movements.

Many of the contributing authors of the series are among the leading scholars and critics of adolescent literature. Some are even young adult novelists themselves. Most of the studies are based on extensive interviews with the subject author, and each includes an exhaustive study of his or her work. Although the general format is the same, the individual volumes are uniquely shaped by their subjects, and each brings a different perspective to the classroom.

The goal of the series is to produce a succinct but comprehensive study of the life and art of every leading young adult author writing in the United States today. The books trace how that art has been accepted by readers and critics, evaluate its place in the developing field of adolescent literature, and—perhaps most important—inspire a reading and re-reading of this quality fiction that speaks so directly to young people about their life's experience.

PATRICIA J. CAMPBELL, GENERAL EDITOR

Preface

I first met Paula Danziger in 1983, when she and I were both giving speeches at the annual Society of Children's Book Writers' conference in Santa Monica. I do not know what she thought of *my* speech—about my experiences at Harcourt, where I was Senior Editor—but I thought *she* was one of the best speakers I had ever heard. Tracing her path to the four successful young adult novels she had published so far, she was outrageously, fall-on-the-floor funny. What a flair for drama (relatively rare on the children's book circuit), and what a larger-than-life presence! Her low, husky voice commanded the attention of anyone within earshot.

To be honest, she also struck me as possibly in need of therapy, or maybe more therapy. Her anger was towering, almost out of control. She seemed a troubled soul, full of compassion for others but only unhappiness with herself and a disturbing honesty about it. She talked of Holden Caulfield (the narrator of *The Catcher in the Rye*) as her emancipator and of the healing power of writing and the written word, charming everyone in the banquet hall into fans and friends.

Her speech was so moving that some people were weeping openly, but for me she was almost painful to watch. She seemed to have no barrier against sharing her private torments with 400 strangers. She reminded me of some stand-up comics I had seen who are more angry than funny, and who bare a little too much of their own souls to be really pleasant company.

After the conference, I learned that she was pleasant company indeed. Our dinner together in a Chinese restaurant, with the artist-author Tomie dePaola, was one of the highlights of my publishing career. Paula Danziger is one of those rare people who rise to close-friend intimacy immediately. Up close, I thought she was a superb listener, a great gossiper, wickedly funny, warm, stimulating, and obviously (to my amateur psychologist's mind) a little off-balance. We talked of books and authors and placed bets on how many manuscript submissions I would receive as a result of my speech.

I had at this point read her first novel, *The Cat Ate My Gymsuit*, and much admired it. Honored with awards and stunning sales in paperback (more than a million copies), it had put her at the top with a splash. A few years after this meeting, I had occasion to use its famous opening line ("I hate my father") in a quiz devised for the *New York Times Book Review*.[1]

Nine years after the Santa Monica conference, when Patty Campbell approached me about writing this book, I for some reason was not surprised. This had to be part of some destiny—not to be corny or "New Age" (pronounced, as Danziger does, to rhyme with "sewage"). I do love to be nosy, and here was such a mesmerizing mind to explore—the mind of one of the superstars in children's books—full of who-knew-what secrets. Among lots of other things, I wanted to know the secret of her fabulous success at reaching young people. This book had to be fate. Who would not grab such an opportunity?

So we met again in 1992, on the opposite coast this time. Over popovers in a restaurant near her Manhattan apartment, and during subsequent meetings, she could not have been more generous in letting me pick her brain. We spoke of many things— pain (psychic as well as the major, horrible dental work she was then enduring), parents, illness, triumph, therapy, jokes, the art of writing for teens, and last but not least, shoes. (Famous as a flashy dresser, she buys her shoes eight to ten pairs at a time, fanciful, sequined and beaded, and in every color of the rainbow.)

She seemed much becalmed since our last meeting, just as funny but not nearly so angry and unhappy. The years had made a positive difference: twelve best-selling novels that have established her as a brand-name author, translations of her books into more than a dozen languages, author tours that log up to 50,000 miles a year from Northern Ireland to Australia, young reader medals from Hawaii to New England, her own television show in England, and a glamorous existence that included an apartment on the Upper West Side, a house in Woodstock, New York, and a good part of the year in London.

My last glimpse of her during this visit was a mixture of the glamorous and the painful. A thunderstorm broke open the skies, and as we were both off to other appointments, she helped me out by sharing her car service—my first experience with getting around New York by anything other than the subway. It seemed at the time the height of luxury, truly "Lifestyles of the Rich and Famous YA Authors."

As we parted company, though, I felt a sympathetic twinge of pain in my jaw—because while I was off to meet an editor for lunch, Paula Danziger was on her way not to an author signing, not to a session with publicists and photographers, not even to a fitting for a new sequined cape. She was off to yet another ordeal with the dentist.

Chronology

1944   Paula Danziger is born 18 August in Washington, D.C.

1955   Moves to Metuchen, New Jersey.

1964   For eight of the next ten years, attends Middlebury College's Bread Loaf Writers Conference in Vermont as auditor, contributor, and staff librarian.

1967   Receives B.A. in English, Montclair State College, New Jersey. Three summers as playground supervisor in Metuchen. Completes one summer of graduate work at the Bread Loaf School of English, Middlebury, Vermont.

1967–1971   Teaches English in Edison, Highland Park, Newark, and West Orange junior high schools, New Jersey.

1970   Seriously injured in two car accidents, April.

1971   Begins writing *The Cat Ate My Gymsuit*.

1972–1978   Counselor, coordinator of tutorial services, and supervisor of reading faculty at Montclair State College.

1973   Receives M.A. in Reading, Montclair State College, New Jersey, with emphasis on urban education, group dynamics, and leadership training.

1974–1976   Freelance reader for Dell Publishing Company.

1974   Publishes *The Cat Ate My Gymsuit*.

1978   Publishes *The Pistachio Prescription*.

1979   Publishes *Can You Sue Your Parents for Malpractice?* Becomes full-time writer. Begins spending part of the year in New York City and part in Woodstock, New York.

1980   *There's a Bat in Bunk Five.*

1984   *The Divorce Express.*

1985   *It's an Aardvark-Eat-Turtle World.*

1986   *This Place Has No Atmosphere.*

1987   *Remember Me to Harold Square.*

1989   *Everyone Else's Parents Said Yes.*

1990   *Make Like a Tree and Leave.*

1991   *Earth to Matthew.* Begins appearing on BBC-TV in England.

1992   *Not for a Billion Gazillion Dollars.* Begins dividing time between London, New York City, and Woodstock.

1994   *Amber Brown Is Not a Crayon* and *Thames Doesn't Rhyme with James.*

1995   *You Can't Eat Your Chicken Pox, Amber Brown.*

1. Survival Through Humor (1944–1969)

Proof that Paula Danziger's funny bone never sleeps: Once, while having some agonizing periodontal work done, she astonished her periodontist with her wit. She was, he said, the only patient who had ever gotten out of his chair while cracking a joke. It was even a *dental* joke, and it made him laugh.

What he did not realize, however, is that while in the chair *and* in pain she had shaped a whole book (about her newest character, Amber Brown). She did not just do this in her head, but had gone so far as to jot a few notes on paper—"you know, that paper they mix the gunk on," she explains.[1]

Here, then, is proof that Paula Danziger's writing instincts never rest. It is this combination of pain and humor—and writing about both—that sums up her whole life. And to understand her books, and why teenagers find them so appealing, it is perhaps more than usually necessary to know about this author's life. "My books sound like I'm talking all the time," Danziger admits.[2] More so than most authors for young adults, her presence—vital, silly, and compassionate—pervades her written work.

She was born on August 18 in 1944 in Washington, D.C., while her father was stationed in Hawaii. Her mother sent him a telegram: "DAUGHTER BORN PLEASE DON'T WORRY," which Danziger finds alternately amusing and ominous. She was not to see her father for her first eighteen months. When he returned, they moved to Nutley, New Jersey, where her brother Barry was born, lived for a while on a farm in Pennsylvania (perhaps the source of her lack of enthusiasm for animals), and then moved to Metuchen, New Jersey, when she was in sixth grade.

Danziger claims that she has known since second grade that she wanted to be a writer: "While other kids had imaginary playmates, I had a follow-the-dot kingdom. I had the magic pencil, *with* the magic eraser, and this whole town was dependent on me. If they wanted a dog or cat they had to come to me, and I'd draw the dots. I'd make their houses for them, extra playmates. If I got angry and didn't like them, I'd erase them." It was a "real control thing," she admits now, "and it's also what I do today— it's what writers do."

She also somehow knew that writing would bring success within her lifetime—no pathetic garret life for her. By third grade she had started practicing her autograph. Wanting to become packaged as a "boxed set" was an early goal.

Thinking back to that time, Danziger says, "I don't ever remember not having books in my hand." She has her mother, who bought books for her and read to her every day, to thank: "My earliest memory is of going to the library. Sometimes my mother would shop and leave me there, and I'd have a book finished by the time she got back. The librarian was wonderful— when I read all the children's books she moved me into the adult section."

The first book she recalls loving was *The Little Engine that Could*: "I still use that line, 'I think I can, I think I can, I know I can' before anything that makes me nervous—a speech or a big date or doing a TV show."

Danziger read quickly and was soon polishing off at least six books a week: "I loved books—they were a way to get out of my life. If it had print on it I read it." That meant comics (about Little Lulu, Archie, Jughead, and Veronica, and superheroes), her mother's nursing books, and her father's law books. The Landmark books helped her with history lessons and were among the few nonfiction books with which she persisted. Her preference was fiction, including science fiction—books by Isaac Asimov and Ray Bradbury. She read all the Nancy Drew and Hardy Boys books, as well as the Cherry Ames and Sue Barton nurse stories. She sees no problems with teenagers reading series books and "just laughs" when people get upset about it.

Betty Smith's *A Tree Grows in Brooklyn* was probably the first "YA" (book for young adults) she ever read, or perhaps Louisa May Alcott's *Little Women* or Herman Wouk's *Marjorie Morningstar*. "But I think the first YA ever *written* was Jane Austen's *Pride and Prejudice*," she comments (and the racy plot summary she offers to her audiences now proves irresistible—"I want that book, I want that book!" the teenagers plead).

It was in high school that she discovered J. D. Salinger's *The Catcher in the Rye*: "And that was my book. I read it every day for three years. I just felt I wasn't alone, there was hope for me. It's when I knew I could be a writer."

Already writing was coming to seem her salvation: "I remember growing up and having my father yell at me and thinking *while* he was yelling, 'That's okay, sometime you can use this in a book.'" Even as a child, she was somehow able to make that amazing leap—the sign of a born writer—of realizing that what may be misery in the present could make good material in the future. Thoughts like this were a way of getting through pain, of getting something out of it, of even making it pay.

Danziger, it seems, always has been a person who feels things deeply. Even today, she says, "I sometimes feel like the character Guilietta Masina plays in Fellini's movie *La Strada*." The face of the naïve, abused young girl—"so hurt and betrayed—with that raw open pain. It's the look of a child. You can never be as hurt as you are when you're a child and you don't know you have defenses."

And by the time Danziger hit adolescence, she was in pain, angry and confused. The anger came from her family life: "Now it would be called 'dysfunctional'—that pop psychology word. Back then we were just the Danzigers," she quips. She can joke about it now: "We were a nuclear family only in the sense of being explosive."

It was hard to see the humor at the time: "There was always tension in my house." Alcohol was not a factor, as her parents did not drink: "But I've been to Adult Children of Alcoholics [a self-help group for people whose parents were alcoholics] meetings because my parents were 'dysfunctional' in some of the same ways—they acted just like alcoholics except without the alcohol." (Danziger has been known to describe herself as an "adult child," which in its way could help explain her success with teenagers.)

Danziger perceived the source of the tension as her father: "He had a very bad temper. He never hit, just yelled. His word was law, and if you disagreed you got screamed at and demeaned. My mother was weak and couldn't stand up to him." Danziger in turn picked on her three-years-younger brother. It is said that siblings can have entirely different childhoods; certainly Barry Danziger had different experiences than Paula and disagrees with much of what she says about her parents.

Danziger's relationship with her father, who died about twelve years ago, was stormy and complex. She calls him "a smart man"—he liked wordplay, he could be "hysterically funny," and he was a fan of comedy. "His favorite comic was Jackie Gleason, and that was also my father's type of humor, the put-down kind." To this day she cannot watch old Gleason shows: "I can't take all that screaming and yelling—too much like my own house."

Her father worked in the garment district as a sales manager, though he had a law degree. For years Danziger blamed herself for being the cause of his not using his degree, as he made a point of saying that practicing law was too risky with a wife and children to support.

Danziger now feels that her father was damaged and scarred from his own growing-up years: "I don't think he was ever happy." His family was first-generation immigrant (grandparents on both sides of her family came from Poland and Russia). Some of his family had escaped from Poland before World War II and some had not; many died in concentration camps. His own mother was "not crazy about him, from what I've heard, not supportive. He wasn't well treated but didn't know how to talk about it." His was a family that did not show love easily. To his daughter he seemed arbitrary and volatile: "You never knew what you were going to be yelled at for or when, when you were going to be put down."

There was at least one predictable sore spot: "It caused a lot of trouble with my father if you showed you were smart," she says. "All you had to do was say you didn't agree with something, and my father would yell, 'You think you know everything, you think you're better than everybody else.'" She often took this to heart and was aware of consciously working to keep a C average; at one point teachers told her she had better work her way into the upper half of the class if she ever wanted to get into college.

Then there were contradictions: "I would make cards for him and he would run around showing them off to neighbors." When she started publishing books about some very troubled families, her mother fretted, "People will think Paula had a difficult childhood," to which her father reportedly replied, "She probably did, but look what she made out of it"—which to Danziger showed that he finally understood. But at the same time, the overall feeling remained that "nothing I did was ever good enough."

By seventh grade there was plenty of evidence that she was an angry, upset child. The anger was overwhelming—"when you're a kid, you're angry when you realize everything isn't perfect"—and there were many manifestations of it, including overeating: "I turned my anger in and did things to punish myself." The family doctor, rather than seeing any of this as a cry for help—"that would have been admitting problems in the 'Ozzie and Harriet' land of suburban New Jersey"—prescribed tranquilizers for Danziger, who was then twelve years old.

Something that not many people know about Danziger is that she has had bulimia—an eating disorder that involves a compulsive binge-purge pattern. Her method of choice for purging was vomiting, which can lead to such physical consequences as dental problems, stomach rupture, and troubles with the heart, kidney, and liver. Among bulimia's other effects on Danziger, it has helped to ruin her teeth: "It brings the acids up from your stomach and destroys the enamel," she says by way of explaining all the major dental work she has endured years later. ("Sugar didn't help either," she adds.)

This behavior was "not what I did to lose weight, it was something I did when I was most angry at myself." She never talked about it or her family problems with her friends: "This was an era when you kept your problems in your own house," she says. Devastating eating disorders such as bulimia were never mentioned in the 1950s; they are only just being talked about today, when it has been estimated that they affect some four percent of young women. Danziger sees now that talking would have helped: "That's why people are bulimics—they *don't* talk about this stuff."

She thinks it is important to mention it now: "I like to talk about bulimia in terms of survival. I don't want to be 'goopy' and have people say, 'Oh, isn't she a survivor.' But I want kids to know that you can grow out of it, that if you have this as an issue, you have to get help." The process of recovery can be a long one, involving nutritional counseling, psychotherapy, and medication.

It was years before Danziger got direct help with bulimia, but in the meantime she did have her strength, weapon, and trademark: her sense of humor. "Humor," declares Danziger, "is emotional chaos remembered in tranquility." It is a line borrowed from James Thurber (and ultimately from Wordsworth's definition of poetry as "emotion recollected in tranquility"), and a quote she has been fond of since using it in *The Pistachio Prescription*.[3] Humorists from Mark Twain ("The secret source of Humor itself is not joy but sorrow"[4]) to Lenny Bruce ("All my humor is based on destruction and despair"[5]) might agree.

Survival through humor is Danziger's recurring theme in her books as well as her life—"it's a way to deal with sadness in life." She grew up liking the comedians and the comic programs of the 1950s, such as Ernie Kovacs and *Show of Shows*." While other kids her age had crushes on Elvis Presley and Ricky Nelson, she had a crush on comedian Mike Nichols: "I loved Elaine May and Mike Nichols's comedy albums."

She knew she could make herself laugh a lot—and others, too. "Apparently I was funny as long as anyone could remember," she says frankly. She did not see the power of her humor at the time, but now she realizes it was a way to cope: "When you're funny, you can get very important and angry things out in a smart way that makes others laugh. People either get it or they don't, but you've said it and that matters."

Something else that made "an incredible difference" to her during this time was the existence of relatives outside the immediate family with whom she was able to spend time. Aunts and uncles took her to plays and concerts and "let me know there was a world outside." One uncle was soft-spoken and gentle, in direct contrast to how she perceived her father; another was a beatnik her father said she would turn out like if she was not careful. One particularly close aunt was an art teacher, who was dramatic and creative and treated her almost as a daughter.

It had to have helped Danziger visualize ways out of her situation to see that her mother worked outside the home earlier than most mothers at that time, starting when Paula was in sixth grade. The other side of this coin was that, since her mother was a nurse at various points (and eventually a therapist for children with cerebral palsy), "You did real well if you were sick—you got a lot of attention. I was out of school a lot, with real stuff and hypochondria."

School, at least after a certain point, was not a great source of stimulation for her. She claims she stopped liking it in sixth grade: "I had a tyrannical teacher who was so mean that my mother even went in to talk to her." There was no such thing as a class in creative writing: "These were the days of *Sputnik* and science—couldn't let the Russians beat you." She was rebellious and "for some teachers I wasn't easy to handle, because I asked questions all the time." She remembers getting a lot of detention "for talking." She also recalls "hearing about a high school newspaper adviser who said after I had stormed out of a room: 'You know, when you're as creative as Paula sometimes you have to give 'em a little leeway.'"

She used to get A's over F's on papers: "I would turn in something really good; it just wasn't what the assignment was." She admits, however, that she did attend good suburban schools, and in high school, seminars brought in drama critics from New York and other speakers who expanded her horizons. She was art editor on the *Bulldog Bark*, the high school paper (and always wonders if she should have gone on in art). She did want to be feature editor, "but you had to do headline counts and they were so *boring*."

During her senior year, as it came time for college, Danziger's father quit his job and decided to go into real estate. The timing of his decision—which left no money for college—made her angry: "It hit me out of left field, just so painful." She got a scholarship to Montclair State Teachers College and worked her way through, with some parental help later on, and earned a bachelor's degree in English.

Once she got to college, her wraparound skirts kept coming untied, she flunked earth science and gym, and professors kept saying, "If only you were an art major we could understand you." When asked to describe her most embarrassing moment, she says, "It was one of the longest moments ever, lasting from the time I was thirteen until I was nineteen." At one point she spent six months with a brace on her leg and eventually had to have surgery on it (which in part explains her exuberance with footwear today—to compensate for the times when braces and casts were all she could wear).

She was, however, editor of *Galumph*, the campus humor magazine, and never seems to have lost her ambition. She envisioned publication in the *New Yorker* by age twenty-one (and snagging the Pulitzer Prize by thirty). Recently, a college friend reminded her of a conversation they once had: "I said, 'Someday I'm going to be rich and famous,' and my friend said, 'Someday I'm going to be anonymous'"; her friend pointed out that they had both got what they wanted.

"Not that I'm really rich," Danziger demurs, "and I'm not really famous, except maybe in England." But the dream was still there, in college, albeit not in clear focus yet.

Encouragement came from a familiar source: "Libraries and librarians have saved my life so many times," says Danziger. It was in college that a librarian introduced her to the first and most important of her mentors—the American poet John Ciardi. Poetry editor and columnist for the *Saturday Review* for many years, Ciardi wrote essays on poetry, compiled volumes of his own poems, translated such works as Dante's *The Divine Comedy*, and directed the Bread Loaf Writers Conference for sixteen years.

John Ciardi and his wife Judith hired Danziger as a "monster-minder," or baby-sitter for their three children, and she was able to travel with them to places like the Bread Loaf Conference: "I practically moved in with them, had free run of their library, spent holidays there—they had a Christmas stocking with my name on it—and through them met writers like Shirley Jackson and Howard Nemerov and Archibald MacLeish."

Most of all, through reading and discussing Ciardi's poetry, especially his work for children, she was truly awakened to the world of words. His children's poems were witty and perceptive, not saccharine as was the fashion of the times. As one obituary stated at his death: "[Ciardi] was outspokenly critical of traditional poetry aimed at youngsters, which struck him as 'written by a sponge dipped in warm milk and sprinkled with sugar.'"[6]

Danziger learned that playing with language was a joyous thing, "and that the more I did it, the more it was appreciated." Ciardi encouraged her on a professional level to think of herself as smart and talented, and on a personal level to express herself. "I grew up with a father who had trouble showing feeling, and here was John knocking on our doors, all excited to tell me and the kids to come look at the raccoons outside."

After college, however, Danziger went on to the career her parents expected of her: teaching. She taught English in Edison, Highland Park, Newark, and West Orange schools. Her special talents blossomed when teaching eighth and ninth grade, and the good news was that "I found out I was terrific with kids." The mixed news was that "I was not real structured as a teacher. I once said to a class, 'Do you know what improvisation is?' and one boy said, 'Yes—what you do in class every day.'" Taking attendance was a hit-or-miss affair; lesson plans were ignored; keys to her classrooms went missing.

Even her clothes lacked a certain structure, as on the day when her half-slip, its elastic having snapped, fell to her ankles and nearly caused a riot. Another day, she wore a pants outfit despite a dress code that forbade pants on female teachers (and then had to wear just the tunic part all day).

She apparently was a teacher straight out of a Paula Danziger book: "Another teacher said that he always recognized my students the year after I taught them, because they didn't raise their hands and they didn't always accept what the teacher said." Her anger surfaced at unfairness, such as the time when the valedictorian was not allowed to speak at graduation because his hair was too long. She became a "fire and health hazard" the time she brought in strobe lights and loud music for the Marshall McLuhan lesson. She hung up a six-foot-tall poster of Woody Allen's *Sleeper*.

As one of her last student evaluations read: "This woman should have been locked up years ago but we're glad she wasn't." Kids have been known to tsk-tsk: "You're as bad as we are."

She did bring in lots of books, and when she was adviser to an interracial discussion group in 1969–70, selected John Howard Griffin's *Black Like Me* and the works of one of her favorite poets, Langston Hughes, and had kids make a bulletin board using Martin Luther King Jr.'s quote, "We must live together as brothers or perish as fools."

Kids who were not big readers at the beginning of the year were usually avid ones by the end. She remembers a class that complained about a classic she was trying to teach: "We know you like books about kids with problems, but we just don't want to read a grown-up talking down to us and telling us how to act." These became the first kids in the country to read Robert Cormier's *I Am the Cheese* as a class, for which Danziger was able to obtain advance copies.

Danziger still gets Christmas cards from ex-students. She is not aware of any of them having gone on to vocations in writing, although one has achieved fame as an actor: Ian Ziering of the trendy TV show *Beverly Hills 90210* (see the dedication to *Can You Sue Your Parents for Malpractice?*).

Perhaps Danziger would have endured a long and semi-notorious career as a junior high English teacher. Not one but two random acts of violence in April of 1970 intervened, and they changed the course of her life.

2. Let the Writing Begin (1970–1994)

"I was stopped at a stop sign," Danziger begins, "and a police car came up from behind and rammed my car into the intersection." She suffered serious whiplash, and a mere six days later she had another accident: a drunk driver slammed into her car head-on. Wearing a seat belt saved her life, but she did go through the windshield with the left side of her head. "The plastic surgeon did a great job. There are a hundred stitches in my face."

Outwardly the scars were minor; inside was a different story. She began to have trouble reading. She lost the ability to write (except backward) and to type. She had no memory of the actual crash. She could not drive easily; she could not even go up steps without falling. After a brain scan, doctors told her she had sustained some brain damage—extent unknown.

The news devastated her. Before the accident she was living an independent life at age twenty-five: "I had an apartment with a whole bunch of people. We called it the anticommune commune—not all of us got along." Now, being in the hospital for weeks made her feel helpless, and worse yet was having to move back in with her parents temporarily. Feelings about her father and "childhood stuff" were brought to the fore. The drugs she was given, for these injuries and unrelated medical problems that same year, were disorienting.

She somehow made it to the end of the school year—students had been coming to see her in the hospital in groups of ten to fifteen—but then she had to quit teaching. When she began having constant nightmares about being hit from the back and the front

11

and her head snapping off, she knew it was time to confront some lifelong problems head-on: "I was dealing with a lot of issues about growing up and feeling out of control."

Danziger had been to psychologists before, but not seriously, until now. She found the experience "incredibly liberating"— despite its inauspicious beginning (at their first meeting she drove over the therapist's front lawn by mistake, and so the first time he saw her she was hysterical). It was while seeing this therapist that she began writing *The Cat Ate My Gymsuit*. If she was ever going to be a writer, she decided, the time was now.

Her therapist did not suggest the book, but he read it in progress. Paula Danziger's writing career had officially begun, and the rest, as they say, is history. *Cat*, the most autobiographical of her books, was her first writing, and unlike just about every other writer in existence, Danziger has never had anything rejected. None of her books has ever gone out of print, and with the exception of her first, all were awarded contracts before she had finished them.

Still, as traumatic as her car accidents had been, did it not scare her to death to write a first book about a family so suspiciously similar to Danziger's own? "Yes, it was terrifying to put things about my family in print," she says now, "but once you've put your head into a windshield and been told you have brain damage, it didn't matter. I just had to get this book on paper. It suddenly became about *just telling the story*." With the publication of *Can You Sue Your Parents for Malpractice?*, her third novel, in 1979, Danziger was a full-time writer, needing no other means of support.

Meanwhile, she still felt incapable of teaching, and so she went back to graduate school, to Montclair State College for her master's degree in reading. It was perhaps there, in her creative writing class or her course on Literature for Adolescents, that she encountered the writers for young adults who influenced her or with whom she is usually categorized; she learned that "there was more to the field than 'Barbie gets acne, triumphs over it to become homecoming queen and the girlfriend of the captain of the football team.'"[1]

She does not recall reading Judy Blume, the writer she is most frequently compared to, at this early stage, although she could have; *Are You There God? It's Me, Margaret* came out in 1970, *Then Again, Maybe I Won't* in 1971. She admires Blume's books and recalls that Blume was one of the first people she met once she started doing author tours: "I met her even before my first book came out." (The Danziger family in Blume's *Forever*, incidentally, is named after a pharmacist in Elizabeth, New Jersey, not Paula.) Danziger adores the Ramona stories of Beverly Cleary, but she does not think she read them at this point either, but rather later.

The one writer (besides J. D. Salinger) who she can say with certainty influenced her was Louise Fitzhugh, an author she very much admires. *Harriet the Spy* (1964), the funny, touching story of an eleven-year-old budding writer, was the only book around that was the kind of book Danziger envisioned for herself. It is a classic portrait of an outsider, acute in its depiction of the anger and angst of the psychologically abused child. Like many of Danziger's books, it combines anger and humor to make a witty work of art that appeals to generation after generation.

As for the writers for young adults she has come to like since she started publishing, Lois Lowry and her Anastasia books rank perhaps the highest. "I love a book if it's funny and bright and caring and honest," Danziger declares. E. L. Konigsburg is another favorite—"she reinvents herself with every book." She likes Bruce Coville, Avi, Brock Cole, Patricia Hermes, Daniel Pinkwater (*Author's Day* in particular), and Gary Paulsen—"though his books are not like mine, very boy, not my neighborhood." Danziger and Paulsen may both write survival stories, but, she says, "my idea of survival in the wilderness is not staying at the Beverly Wilshire Hotel, so Gary Paulsen and I will probably never write the same books." She also admires Katherine Paterson—"though we don't write alike." Patricia Reilly Giff is another favorite—"very funny and very moving."

Danziger is friends with many writers, some famous and some she hopes will become better known. Rather than relying on writers' groups, she uses her friends as individual sounding boards, and vice versa. She and Bruce Coville have read several of each others' manuscripts to each other page by page, and she has also read books aloud to Pat Giff. It is an important writing technique to her to read a manuscript aloud over the phone—"It works better than in person; I don't know why."

Sometimes writer-friends fulfill more unusual roles: "This is so shallow and not grown-up, but when I start a book I put a piece of jewelry away and I'm not allowed to get it till I finish the book. It becomes a symbol—I could show you a watch or a pair of earrings for practically each book I've done. Though there have been a couple of books I've written for the sheer joy of writing!" Famous friends help out: "Francine Pascal [of *Sweet Valley High* fame] holds jewelry for me—she's tough, she doesn't even let me see it much. Ann M. Martin [best-selling author of the *Babysitters' Club* series] is now holding a beautiful necklace that she won't hand over till I finish—as close a friend as she is, she's unrelenting."

Some of the best writing being done today is for children or young adults, Danziger believes. Among her favorite writers for the older set are Anne Tyler, Toni Morrison ("absolutely brilliant"), Dick Francis (she likes his writing though she does not care much for mysteries or horse races), and of course, writers who make her laugh: Calvin Trillin, Russell Baker, Dave Barry, and Mark Twain. (And she still pursues comedy—"I love that play with words"—into clubs and on TV; some of her favorite comedians now are Rita Rudner, Tracy Ullman, and Emo Phillips. Female comics who disparage themselves, cruel humor, and "shock-jocks" are distinctly unappealing.)

As for writers whom she herself has influenced, Danziger professes not to keep track of imitators: "I'm sure there are people who say, 'I want to write a funny book with feeling,' but then it becomes their own book." She has seen reviews that refer to "a book like Paula Danziger's," and an editor did once ask her to "Danzigerize" a manuscript, but she has not spent time keeping score or analyzing her influence.

Danziger has worked with a variety of editors during her career; some of them she liked, some she did not. Perhaps surprisingly for one who stresses that "editors make a big difference," she does not always remember the names of editors on each book: "I call it Danziger's Theory of Living: You can only keep so much in your brain. I've had to give up state capitols, the names of everyone who was mean to me in junior high (except for two people), and other names, dates, and places." A bad editor for her is nitpicky in a wrongheaded way (*"good* three-page letters are okay").

A good editor has her sense of play (she has been known to teach editors to play video games), an understanding of comic timing, and an awareness of what Danziger calls "the Ciardi purple." This comes from Ciardi's analysis of a particularly influential poem (John Frederick Nims's "Love Poem"): "He said that if you underlined its funny lines in red and the serious lines in blue, you would end up with purple—the combination of the sad and funny."

Danziger is the only writer she knows who is told to make things *less* funny. She claims that editors have worked hard "to get me not to cover everything with jokes, which is what I did with my life. In the very beginning an editor kept me from going for the joke too easily." Good editors, she adds, "have been right in what they've crossed out. Sometimes editors are on a different planet from me, but that doesn't mean they can't come up with good stuff."

It almost goes without saying that she prefers an editor she likes to spend time with: "I need someone I can talk to, who has a sense of who I am—otherwise I'm on edge right away." An editor once told her her nails were too long: "You're not working hard enough if your nails are that long." Psychic editors are good; one of them would stick a Post-It on a manuscript page with no comment and Danziger would always know what needed to be changed. Gill Evans, her current British editor, gets read aloud to on a daily basis whenever Danziger is in England. Editors have even helped her through personal crises. Last but not least, "A good editor makes sure you get your advance the second you finish your book."

Her current American editor, Margaret Frith, is simpatico: "She told me the other day, 'I can tell, it's going to be just like with Jean Fritz, I'm going to tell the copy editor to just find the mistakes if there are any, but don't touch your style. You're very *sure* of what your style is and why you have chosen each word.'"

"I really am," Danziger acknowledges, "and people are surprised by that. They think because I'm funny that it was easy, but I know why words were chosen. I know where I'm going and there's a straight line. It may change but I go back and rework it. I write and rewrite a lot. A book may sound like me talking, but it took hard work to get it that way."

In addition to reading her work aloud, Danziger has also learned about writing from studying acting. An early mentor urged her to read *Respect for Acting* by Uta Hagen and take acting lessons. She studied with the actor Brad Dourif (most famous for his role in *One Flew Over the Cuckoo's Nest*) for a year, and the experience helped her growth as a person and a writer: "I learned so much about myself. And I laughed—I had to leave class one night I was laughing so hard."

One acting technique in particular helped: "When you go in, you know what the character wants more than anything else—all else happens around that. I use that all the time; it's very defined for me, and not only for the main character." Danziger now believes that if she had understood more about motivation when she was writing *Cat*, "it would have been a better book. The father would have been more rounded if I had understood what he felt emotionally from his own deprived, angry childhood."

Danziger now tries to know as much about her characters as possible, using a "webbing technique" to work information in, but also deciding things about each character (what secrets are hidden in his closet, what is her favorite breakfast, what posters are on his wall, what is her least favorite outfit) that do not necessarily make it into the final manuscript. And she takes personally a quotation from Constantin Stanislavsky (whose techniques revolutionized modern acting): "Love the art in yourself, not yourself in the arts."

Acting lessons helped in yet another way, in what has become all but a second career for Danziger: speaking. Almost as important to her career as John Ciardi was Jerry Weiss, a professor at

Montclair State College and editorial consultant to Dell Publishers (and to whom *There's a Bat in Bunk Five* is dedicated). Besides championing *Cat* at Dell, he made sure she got "on the road," lining her up for speaking engagements at conferences. She quickly developed a reputation for being a flamboyantly funny speaker and became much in demand in schools and at conventions as "comic relief." Her lack of inhibition works to her advantage: "I tell more than most. I don't have that funnel that stops most people from being too open." Danziger has had people come up and say, "I've heard you speak ten times" (to which she says, "My God, I can't stand hearing myself that much"). Still, there are always new people, those who have not yet heard her most famous story (the day her slip fell down).

Her needs as a speaker are minimal: a Diet Pepsi ("though that's not always good because you burp after it"); no uncooked tomatoes in anything (they swell up her throat so that she cannot talk); and not getting picked up in the morning by people she does not know: "I'm enough of a New Yorker to think they're going to kidnap me and don't know I've spent all my money on shoes."

Paula Danziger is such a funny speaker that she is often asked why she did not go into stand-up comedy. She has a response at the ready: "I *would* have become a stand-up comic except that I have trick knees [a hereditary medical problem that causes her joints to slip out of socket] and I'm a morning person, so I had to find something else."

Unlike many writers of the quiet and retiring kind, Danziger genuinely enjoys speaking. One of her writer-friends, Pam Swallow, once took Danziger and Ann M. Martin to see a performance of Spalding Gray's *Monster in a Box.* Inside the little theater, they were looking around, with Ann characteristically thinking how terrifying it would be to perform here, Pam checking for the fire exit . . . and Danziger marveling, "My God, what a *wonderful* place this would be to speak."

Partly, she says, "It's the ex-teacher in me. It fills a need. I learn a great deal, help other people—and get a chance to wear new clothes. Plus I just like it. I feel like there's a net: I'm there as a writer and I don't *have* to be funny." But because she has such a "high sense of funny," there has been no need for the net.

"I *am* one of the funniest people I know," Danziger does not mind saying. "I laugh when I'm writing—I love it when that happens. I have a 'funny focus,' and when it's going well nothing else matters." Humor to her is not discipline: "I don't think I'm very disciplined." A professor in college once told her she "flitted from thing to thing sort of like a butterfly going for things that were bright and shiny." Another told her she was not a great scholar, which she now cheerfully admits.

She usually does not outline or plot books in advance. "My strength is not plot," she acknowledges. She does not keep notebooks—"I'm not good at that." She tries to write things down, but she tends to lose them. But she does have a knack for keeping things in her brain. She is constantly eavesdropping in restaurants and shops for bits she might be able to use in a book ("I'm curious; I'm very nosy"); constantly making up jokes in her head; constantly weighing whether a piece of material is good or *great*.

Unlike most authors, she can go for months without writing while she is processing material. "I spend a long time thinking about a book before I put it down on paper," she says, "and I watch a lot. I spend a long time just watching." She has been known to ride buses in New York just to hear how kids talk. But she firmly believes that "a writer writes every day whether or not there's a pen in hand." And in part her relatively small output is a function of pain; it hurts her fingers to write. At times during her career, her books have been spaced several years apart, a longer-than-average span for the top young adult authors.

One technique that she learned from a lecture by Shirley Jackson (most famous for *The Lottery*) has proven useful: "You don't just put something in a book once; you bring it back again. If I put something in the beginning, you know it's going to show up later, because then it's got a value and a memory." Jackson also said to "call it what it really is. If your heroine's hair is golden call it yellow. I still go for the easy joke sometimes, but even the easy jokes have to do with that character's character." Her advice to new authors is "to get yourself calm and clear so it comes out on the page."

One amazing fact about Danziger is that it does not matter to her where she is when she writes. Besides being capable of making notes in the dentist's chair, she writes on planes, in restaurants, and once wrote a book in locations all over London. B.C. (Before Computers), she wrote in longhand lying in bed on her stomach, with her legs up like a junior high kid, and then transferred the drafts to a typewriter.

Now she uses a laptop computer and often writes in her living room on a TV tray. Only once did she ever have real trouble writing, or writer's block, and then it was partly a matter of ergonomics: she eventually realized her desk was too high, having been built for a six-foot-four-inch tall man.

All this writing, says Danziger, has allowed her to get over being so angry. But there is another, one-word, answer to how she got rid of the anger: "therapy." She has not been in regular therapy for several years, but there is no question that it changed her life. For one thing, she seems fearless now, but she spent years being afraid of everything, with phobias both rare and common. She hated escalators, elevators (and would always take a book inside, in case of breakdowns), *and* stairs (convinced that a fall would kill her). Traveling brought dangers: "I personally concentrated on keeping the plane up in the air and on it making a safe landing. I also willed trains to stay on the track."[2] She still has to put on her shoes in a certain order, and she is also hypochondriac in some ways: "I recently got a bee sting and thought I might die. The adrenaline hits me in a thirty-cups-of-coffee way and lasts for a day."

She also has real health problems: allergies (including asthma), a thyroid condition, and an oversupply of collagen. "That's why my joints go out of socket—where normal people would break, I go out of socket. It's required two operations on one leg and one on my shoulder. But it's also why my skin doesn't wrinkle so much!"

Most of the effects of her two car accidents, however, turned out to be temporary. It was not until years later that Danziger learned that she did not have brain damage from the accidents, but rather that some of her problems were a result of the collagen surplus, an inherited syndrome. The number of drugs Danziger was put on during that time has made her very anti-drug, both in life and in her books: "It takes a lot for me to take aspirin at this point."

Having been given tranquilizers in the seventh grade, though, has made her interested in medicine ever since. Today she talks so expertly about bodywork, massage, biofeedback, acupuncture, and other aspects of holistic medicine (in which she has taken courses) that she is sometimes assumed to be from California (where she would never live—"too many earthquakes"). "I think maybe writers are healers, too," she muses, "because you allow other stuff to come out when people read you."

She has never written about her accidents, nor bulimia, nor other subjects she considers just too painful: "I had a friend who died of AIDS and asked me to write a book, a YA dealing with AIDS with humor. I just can't detach myself that much, and luckily it's been written—*Two Weeks With the Queen* by Morris Gleitzman—which I publicize wherever I can." Nor can she write about the Holocaust, except briefly in *Remember Me to Harold Square*.

Perhaps the biggest reason for her worldwide success is her gift for looking at events through the eyes of someone who is thirteen, fourteen, or fifteen years old. "People have said to me it's wonderful how I come down to kids' level," she says. "I think that's appalling. I don't come down to kids' level. I respond on a level I feel comfortable on." A teen perspective usually happens to be the same as hers: "I'm not like most grown-ups," she admits.

In some aspects of her life Danziger still *is* a child. She loves pinball (it "should be in every reading lab in the country because it teaches good hand-eye coordination") and video games, plays jacks on the floor, carries Winnie-the-Pooh bandages in her purse, and has an enormous collection of stickers (she uses them to personalize answers to fan mail). "A guy I once dated used to tease me about hiding a child," she says—" 'I just know you have one, with all the toys around.'"

Some days, indeed, Danziger much regrets not having children. "But if I had kids I wouldn't have the freedom to travel the way that I do. A child's love is responsibility, and I lead a peripatetic life; I like being able to pick up and go. Also I've always felt unprepared to be a parent. If I had a child I would have to put away money for therapy. Or else I'd have a kid who wanted to work for IBM and he'd complain, 'You're always bringing me crayons and taking me to plays!'"

Danziger also has some (but not a lot of) regrets that she never married. "I used to be afraid that if I ever got really involved I'd have to cook and clean and not be who I really was. I decided early on what can work here—I can write, live my life, work some of this childhood stuff out so I understand it—and I've been able to do some of that." Now she wonders if being a writer is incompatible with marriage (except to another writer—"but then creative people can be problematic").

"There are certain things I do well," Danziger quips. "I find great parking places, but I'm not good in relationships." Seriously, she says, "I wasn't good at finding people who were good for me. I rarely make mistakes in judgment—except about dates." In part she takes responsibility: "I was never available emotionally to make it work." And partly she faults her childhood: "I had no examples of interactions with people being kind and loving, though they may have tried. My parents were not monsters, just people of their background. But I think I was so damaged in so many ways that I couldn't extend out of myself enough."

At this point, she says, "the whole idea of marriage is not as important to me. It would be nice to find somebody to play with and to be there for the difficult times. But I like what I'm doing— I've lived alone a long time and my life is pretty complete. If I end up never marrying I'll be fine, if lonely sometimes, but then I know a lot of lonely married people."

Danziger has thought a lot about adopting kids alone, especially older kids, and the idea of stepchildren also appeals: "I've always joked that I wanted to find a widower with two kids who was an orphan." Meanwhile, she says, "I love my friends who have kids. And I have friends who *are* kids, which meets a lot of my needs."

Sometimes her kid-friends act as consultants or even work for her. Danziger is deluged with so much fan mail that "I can't do it all. I like to hire kids fifteen and up who are sensitive and caring. They read it and get the letters to me that they should." Her mail frequently contains juvenile humor (responding to the sick jokes Danziger is fond of) and fashion commentaries ("like your books, love your shoes"). Once she came back from a trip, and her helper said she had answered a letter from a girl having an urgent relationship crisis. With great trepidation, Danziger asked, "What did you say? Did you sign my name?" When it turned out the letter had been signed from "Paula's secretary," Danziger was relieved—"I loved it!"

Finally, Danziger has proven to be a world-class aunt, one in the mode of the aunts who so influenced her (and also in the mode of one of her favorite writers, Jane Austen). She is close to her three nephews and one niece, and she takes them on trips to London, Toronto, California, Scotland, and to the theater—most recently to see *Joseph and the Amazing Technicolor Dreamcoat*. "I'm grateful to my brother and sister-in-law for having me as part of the family," she says. Her young niece, Carrie, knows her aunt very well: "You're not a grown-up," she tells her, "you're a *teen*!"

One result of living alone, Danziger has discovered, is "incredibly high phone bills—higher than my rent sometimes. It's because I want to talk to my friends, and writers are isolated with what we do." Her life is tied in to the phone—"I have call-waiting, conference calling, fax machines, the works—it's part of living alone."

She is also always on the road: "I travel more than most people, except maybe Steven Kellogg," a fellow children's book author. She has found a great excuse for living in London part-time (besides research—some of her latest books are set there), which is the monthly eight-minute segment she does on a children's BBC-TV show. Because her books are already so popular in England, she was invited there to talk up books—"great books, but not traditional great books. I get *so* excited—I'm *really* proud of it." She organizes her picks under themes with typically Danziger titles, such as Characters that I Wish Were Friends (after Holden Caulfield's desire to call up his favorite authors on the phone); Books that You Thought Would Make You Puke but You End Up Loving (classics like *Pride and Prejudice*); Because They Make You Do School Reports on Us (autobiographical books by people like Roald Dahl and Jean Little); Science Fiction (Margaret Mahy, Robert Westfall); The Ten Weepiest Books Ever (the show that generated the most mail, featuring books like Katherine Paterson's *A Bridge to Terabithia*, Lois Lowry's *A Summer to Die*, and Harper Lee's *To Kill a Mockingbird*); and Graphic Novels (such as Art Spiegelman's *Maus*).

"The ex-teacher in me loves it," Danziger raves. "On a good day I get to tell three million people about great books. I sit on the floor in bookstores around London, happy as a clam. People from all over the country tell me they're reading what I recommend. I'm recognized in the street there, and my autographings take forever." She has been told that, while everyone else looks ten times heavier on TV, she for some reason looks slimmer: "I look happy, I love it so much."

Danziger acknowledges that she has been "luckier" than most writers in that she lives well: "I should have a gazillion dollars by now, but my choice has been to travel and live that kind of life. So I'm not as wealthy as people think I am, but I haven't had to 'work' since 1978. Speaking, especially, has saved me."

In some years she has taken out loans: "I do like immediate gratification, whether it's food, spending, whatever. I live for malls. I'm getting better, but yes, there are those days when I buy eight pairs of spangly shoes. But they're a *necessity*! They bring kids closer. I could justify forever why I bought eight beaded, sequined shoes and a beautiful sequined bag. . . . And I just bought the most beautiful piece of pottery—every time I look at it it does something to me. And I certainly need more jewelry. . . ."

Fortunately, many more Paula Danziger books are in the works. It all started, however, with a girl named Marcy Lewis.

3. The Marcy Lewis Books

The Cat Ate My Gymsuit (1974)

When *Time* magazine published an article about the newest in literary genres—which they termed "suburban social realism"[1]—the lead paragraph used thirteen-year-old Marcy Lewis from New Jersey as a spokesperson: "Sometimes I feel guilty being so miserable, but middle-class kids have problems too."[2]

According to *Time*, Marcy, the unhappy heroine of Danziger's *The Cat Ate My Gymsuit*, personified the perennial theme of young adult literature, which at that moment was experiencing paperback sales increases of up to 300% and 400%. These were books kids were buying for themselves—the mark of genuine popularity. Prominent along with such trailblazers as Judy Blume, Robert Cormier, Norma Fox Mazer, S. E. Hinton, and others was Paula Danziger, whose "slangy precision" about teen angst was being "avidly shared by a growing legion."[3]

As *The Cat Ate My Gymsuit* opens, Marcy Lewis is full of bile: "I hate my father. I hate school. I hate being fat. I hate the principal because he wanted to fire Ms. Finney, my English teacher" (*Cat*, 1). In short, punchy declarative sentences, Marcy goes on to elaborate her catalog of complaints, using it as a smoke screen for her *real* problem: she lives within a shell that keeps her safe and protected, but also passive and bitterly unhappy. She does things like drink a beer at a party just to go along with the crowd, to avoid standing out any more than she is convinced she already does.

Though the expression is never used, Marcy has almost pathetically low self-esteem. In the first few pages, she does let slip some of her talents: she likes creative writing, and she is in the class of "smart kids." But mostly she considers herself a mousy "blob" about to be further cursed with acne, an "idiot," a hideous blimp whom others should be embarrassed to be seen even talking to—suicide would be preferable.

Gym class, with its spotlight on bodies, is excruciating for her. The book's title comes from one of the numerous witty excuses she invents to avoid partaking in gym altogether (it was one of the better excuses Danziger heard during her teaching career). These are used as throwaway lines, partially to indicate Marcy's submerged sense of humor, partially to establish that she has been avoiding gym for so long that no one takes particular notice anymore.

It is easy to locate the major source of Marcy's poor self-image. Her father, Martin, is the type of man who not only calls her "little lady" (*Cat*, 83), but yells insults like "You look like an animal" (*Cat*, 114) and "Why do I have to have a daughter who is stupid and so fat?" (*Cat*, 26). This man terrorizes his wife (who may be president of the PTA but never stands up to him), his four-year-old son (who takes unnatural refuge with his teddy bear, keeping him well stuffed with orange pits), and his thoroughly intimidated daughter. His entrances have the effect of the monster's appearance in a creepy movie: a car door slamming is "a scary sound when you know it means that your father is home" (*Cat*, 47).

He stops short of physical violence, *just* short in one scene, though one night he cruelly disables the car so Marcy and her mother cannot attend a crucial event. His motivation is never particularly clear, except for a certain caveman selfishness: he was an only child and does not like competing with two children for his wife's attention, and he believes that supporting the family gives him the right to have his way at all times.

Miserable, Marcy at her age is hardly in a position to move out, and so for the time being she is trapped, powerless—and furious. The situation may be unique, but what adolescent would not be able to identify with the feeling? (Or adult, for that matter, especially an adult who has just been in two car accidents through no fault of her own?)

Enter Barbara Finney, the new English teacher, an individual among the crowd of faceless, cookie-cutter adults. She wears denim skirts and giant jewelry (a particular love of Marcy's, as you do not need to buy it in the "Chubbies" section), uses innovative teaching methods, and quotes Theodore Roethke: "'Those who are willing to be vulnerable move among mysteries.' Please, let's try to move among mysteries together," she urges her class (*Cat*, 8). She borrows from Marshall McLuhan, Harper Lee, *The Miracle Worker*, Shakespeare, and her classes in group dynamics. Above all, her concern is "people communicating with people" (*Cat*, 8), and in the course of knowing her, Marcy gradually learns how communication is the one path out of her own miserable existence.

Much to Marcy's (and the reader's) shock, Ms. Finney simply disappears from the school one day. The unsympathetic principal, Mr. Stone, has been gunning for her since day one, and he finally finds a solid excuse to get her dismissed: Ms. Finney refuses to say the Pledge of Allegiance during homeroom. It is one too many stands for a new young teacher to take, according to the "establishment" that Mr. Stone represents. Though the actual reason for her refusal is left mysterious until she has a chance to speak near the novel's end, the students never lose faith in her for a minute; they assume the noblest motives for her and the most intolerant motives for the school administration. It turns out that, while considering herself a good American, she does not believe this country *does* offer liberty and justice for all, and until it does, she cannot say the Pledge. In the book (as in life—Danziger has had most movie producers pass on *Cat* because of this part of the plot), her refusal generates controversy and, among her student fans, rage at "the system's" unfairness.

As tempting as it might have been to turn *Cat* into a book about Ms. Finney, Danziger succeeds in keeping Marcy the focus throughout. By the time the Pledge crisis strikes, Marcy is a whole new human being—still overweight, still saddled with a destructive father and a weak mother, but active for the first time in her life. She takes a leading role in defending Ms. Finney (getting herself suspended in the process, but finally standing up to her father—"I'm not always wrong" [*Cat*, 84]), develops several worthwhile friendships, and sees herself as valuable whether she flunks gym or not (she does). The final chapter reveals that she is seeing a psychologist, no longer eats the ice cream her mother (a classic "enabler," to use an Alcoholics Anonymous term that refers to someone who makes it easier for another to engage in addictive behavior) was always feeding her, and is thinking about following Ms. Finney into bibliotherapy, combining counseling and books. First, however, she will tackle adolescence with attitude intact: "Yesterday I looked in the mirror and saw a pimple. Its name is Agnes" (*Cat*, 147).

Cat is a work of fiction, but as mentioned earlier, it is the most autobiographical of all Danziger's works. She has been known to have herself listed as "Marcy Lewis" in the telephone directory. (The last name, as is Danziger's pattern with her major characters, comes from a favorite Jewish comedian, in this case Jerry Lewis.)

With her first novel, she says, "I wrote about what I knew best. I was a fat little teenager from New Jersey who hated school, with a younger brother who stuck orange pits in his bear. I'd been a teacher who had taken stands, and I wanted to write about taking stands, about surviving with a sense of humor." Inspired by writers like Louise Fitzhugh, she aimed for the type of book that her eighth and ninth grade students could relate to. Ms. Finney's techniques parallel sensitivity training methods Danziger tried at one particular school, and Smedley (the after-school club started by Ms. Finney) is named for a roving bookmobile Danziger brought to school.

Most important of all, she drew on her own feelings of raw rage—at social conditions, at parents, and mostly at fathers.

Marcy is so angry in the beginning that it is amazing she is not a physical wreck—or if she is, it is not clear from the text. Danziger has never treated bulimia in a book, though she says now that "the character most likely to have been bulimic would have been Marcy Lewis. But bulimia wasn't talked about in 1970; it was just never mentioned."

Despite the necessary fictionalization, Danziger says that "*Cat* is very much my growing up. It dealt with a lot of my problems and it's a lot angrier than the other books. It was an incredible step then to put these things in print." She calls her father "very much the father in *Cat*," right down to the smelly cigars he constantly smokes that make his daughter cough. After all these years, their troubled relationship still disturbed her, and she felt abused, though "the violence was always verbal. He hit me maybe only once, and then it scared him to death."

Her therapist read chapters as she was doing them, and he helped her deal with issues as they came up. Marcy learns what her creator was perhaps learning at the same time: "Some people will take negative attention as long as it's attention," says Danziger. "You have to learn not to get sucked into that. You can't let them have that power over you."

Interestingly, the much-heralded opening line "I hate my father" (*Cat*, 1) did not come to Danziger until halfway through the writing of the book. When it did, she says, "I cried—a *lot*."[4] Today she believes that her portrait of Martin Lewis is "too severe and one-sided." But it could have been worse—she recalls actually cutting certain lines to tone it down to what appears in print. After the book came out, however, people would point to different passages and insist, "Paula, no father would say that," to which she would reply, "Wanna bet?"

She knows that other people find her portrait all too real. Once, during a school visit, she had a little girl in a class ask, "Did you really hate your father?" After Danziger said "Yes," the girl let out more than a sigh, what seemed to Danziger almost a release. Danziger wanted to tell her, "It's okay; sometimes things don't turn out the way you want them to—it's okay to say that; it frees you"—which echoes a description of the effect *Cat*'s publication had on her: "incredibly liberating."

Certainly the book changed her relationship to her parents: "When I handed a copy to my father, I told him I loved him. It was safe to do that then; I also was older at that point. I said there's going to be things in this book you won't like." But they talked, and he handled it well: "'Healing' sounds too California. . . . But being able to get this out allowed me to see certain things and start standing up for myself and saying what I think."

Years later, she learned from a friend that her father had a habit of entering bookstores and personally making sure that Paula Danziger books were more prominently displayed than Judy Blume books. "So he was proud of me in a way." Danziger would not go so far as to say she made peace with him before he died, but she did "make progress": "It wasn't happily ever after. It did affect other relationships, though I had to learn from writing not to carry that anger."

Not all reactions to *Cat* were positive. One highly critical article called it "the archetypical bibliotherapeutic novel," the sort of book to be condemned because it teaches kids that "reading is primarily a matter of self-recognition." Especially to be abhorred was the *lack* of reality, rather than the reality, of Marcy's world:

> [It is] a weird wish-fulfilling fantasy of a decidedly unrealistic sort—a world where one always gets what one wants, where one is always right about the inadequacies of others, and where one's consciousness of a problem automatically leads to its solution. It is not surprising that young people like such novels, just as it is not surprising that they like Superman or Nancy Drew, which depict reality in the same way.[5]

Lumping *Cat* with Nancy Drew seems unduly harsh and off-base, but in any case such comments seem unfair for being anxious to deny young adults the pleasure of reading about people like themselves—something that adults do all the time. The very act of recognizing one's own feelings in print, especially during the turbulent teen years, can be a profoundly meaningful experience.

Many years and many books later, Danziger can still quote from memory the first line of *Cat*'s review in *Kirkus Reviews*: "'At its worst, this is a trite and trendy saga'—and it goes downhill from there."[6] This would have devastated her, she says, had not a glowing review reached her first. Veronica Geng, writing in the *New York Times Book Review*, called it "snappy, contemporary . . . funny and alive." While horrified at a father "who sets some kind of record for psychological child abuse," Geng praised the realism that alters Marcy's "relationships with boys, her family and herself."[7] Most critical opinion was in line with the *New York Times*. *School Library Journal* called Marcy "an appealing heroine,"[8] and *Booklist* included *Cat* in its "50 titles of literary merit and lasting appeal for a junior high audience" published between 1950 and 1984.[9]

In terms of popular opinion, *Cat* went on to make its author into that rare phenomenon, an overnight success. As the book passed its twentieth anniversary, it sells as well now as it ever did. Probably her best-selling book, it is frequently used in classrooms (which she finds ironic after Ms. Finney's problems within her *own* classroom).

One reason for the book's longevity is its relative timelessness. The book is all human emotion—there is almost no description of place or time period or anything visual. This could be construed as a flaw; on the other hand, it leaves readers free to fill in their own details. The lack of description allows readers to enter Marcy's mind and get on her side quickly. Only occasionally is there a bit of slang ("we all really dug her" [*Cat*, 15] or "plant grass on Mr. Stone" (*Cat*, 66]) that clearly marks this as a product of the 1970s. Otherwise the language is "Danzigerized" J. D. Salinger ("The thing with Ms. Finney is what I want to talk about" [*Cat*, 3]) that wears well.

The way the book pits the individual kid against "the system" is particularly of its time, the early 1970s, but of course it is also timeless. Marcy is continually urged by Mr. Lewis and Mr. Stone to "play by the rules," and even her mother reinforces the pressure: "It's just that it's safer being like everybody else" (*Cat*, 98). There will never come an era when teens are not pressured to conform, and so there will never be a time when rebels like Marcy are not needed as role models.

Marcy, like Holden Caulfield, the narrator of Salinger's *The Catcher in the Rye*, is full of integrity, attractively honest, someone that boys can relate to as well as girls. She is a "smart-aleck" misfit, brimming with that subversiveness that permeates the best children's books: "John Ciardi said my characters are outlaws with things to rebel against, real reasons," says Danziger. "They fight for what they believe in, and kids respond to that." As flip as her creator might be (dedicating the book to Ciardi "because he dedicated a book to me"), she never allows Marcy that flippancy. The language of the novel is polished, honed, and so smooth that the book easily can be read in one sitting, and it is not hard to imagine kids wanting to. All of the major characters are well developed and believable. The fight for Ms. Finney is depicted realistically—it is not a total victory, but this does not diminish Marcy's new self-respect.

The book's message is universal as well as timeless. Not only does Marcy learn what Ms. Finney has to teach, but she even does it in a literary way, the way a future English major should: "[T]o communicate is to begin to understand ourselves and others. She wanted us to be honest in our thinking, and to write well. That's really hard, to be honest and remember things like commas and paragraph structure and stuff like that" (*Cat*, 12–13). It is a message Danziger may well have taken as her own motto.

Not that Danziger thinks of herself as Western Union delivering telegrams: "I don't write message books," she says. "I write to tell the best story I know how to tell. The second you write with a message in mind you get preachy. But I do think it's important for kids to know that childhood is very difficult for everybody. All those people you thought had it together are going through their own stuff too and are in a lot of pain—and if they weren't then they eventually were."

Above all—and despite the pain—*The Cat Ate My Gymsuit* is funny, with the kind of biting, Woody-Allen-ish wit that also wears well. No matter how low Marcy gets, how much forces conspire against her, how much her paranoia has all-too-real causes, she keeps her way with words. Her life may not be easy, but she never fails to put an ironic spin on it. She expresses herself in a lively, appealing manner all but guaranteed to win the reader's sympathy. Even after an abortive and embarrassing kiss from her potential boyfriend, her spirit is irrepressible: "So much for my career as a sex fiend" (*Cat*, 111). Jokes are never gratuitous or allowed to interfere with the misery or the truly heartrending passages. But Marcy never wallows either—she stays light on her feet, and at the end we know her humor makes her very much a survivor.

There's a Bat in Bunk Five (1980)

Popular response to *Cat* was so overwhelming that readers were soon begging for a sequel. And almost as if Danziger wanted to prove emphatically that Marcy Lewis does survive, she went on to oblige her fans. There were, it seemed, still more things left for Marcy to say, and after another two books, Danziger returned to this character, as well as to Ms. Finney and (briefly) Marcy's troubled family.

With *There's a Bat in Bunk Five*, the very first sentence reveals that Marcy's woes are on a considerably smaller scale these days: "If I iron or sew one more name tag on my stuff, I'm going to scream."[10] Not quite so turned in on herself, she is ready to face the world, leaving for upstate New York and summer camp to be a counselor-in-training in a creative arts program run by her old friend Ms. Finney. The chance to live in a place where only her former English teacher knows she was a "fat nobody" is both scary and alluring.

Since *Cat*, Marcy has lost a lot of her anger and apparently a great deal of weight, while gaining some confidence. She and her family have *all* gone for counseling, and while problems remain (she sometimes wishes her father had died from the heart attack he has had), she has matured: "If my life were a novel, it would be one without much plot, just character development" (*Bat*, 5). Her goals now are to "live my own life and become a writer," and in the meantime she just wants to grow up some more, to "develop my character" (*Bat*, 5).

While Marcy turns fifteen during *Bat*, her little brother is suddenly eight, having aged four years to Marcy's two. (Danziger is not proud of these little mathematical glitches, which crop up in her books occasionally, but they are also a source for her jokes: "Boys don't mature *that* fast!") Her brother is off bears and into football. Mrs. Lewis works outside the home and has stopped popping tranquilizers, and her father, while grumpy and unemotional, is making much more of an effort to be human.

The going-off-to-summer-camp theme allows a protagonist to live on his or her own for the first time; it is a tried-and-true plot in books for teens, and there are certain predictable devices. Every camp has a troublemaker, for example, and in this book it is Ginger, a miserable "child of divorce" who acts destructively and alienates everyone—except Marcy, who decides to save her. After all, thanks to her former unhappiness, she is qualified to provide special insight: "Maybe [Ginger's] got a lot of problems that make her act that way," she suggests (*Bat*, 52).

Marcy's effort possibly reflects a "savior" instinct of Danziger's own: "I'm useful when speaking in school systems not only because I write," she says, "but because I'm someone who doesn't fit in. Kids who feel all alone sometimes think there's a chance when they meet someone like me. I reach the outlaws, the lurkers."

In a realistic twist, however, Ginger turns out to be too much for Marcy. She needs professional help, just as Marcy herself did. But through trying to understand her, the older girl learns much: "I used to think that things were the worst in my family. Now I can really see that other people have problems too" (*Bat*, 144).

Marcy's story is like a giant pep talk in fourteen chapters, using various voices (including Marcy's own) to talk herself out of her many fears: meeting new people, doing things on her own, the camp goats, men (will they all yell at her like her father?), getting fat again, not to mention the pesky and possibly rabid bats. The bats symbolize her overriding fear: "Just when things are going well, something happens to ruin it. It's like I'm being punished for being happy and doing what I want to do. That's why I'm so scared much of the time" (*Bat*, 90).

Bat, a novel somewhat light on plot and character development, frequently reads like a motivational package for adolescents, even at one point echoing Danziger's own earliest reading—*The Little Engine that Could*: "I can do it. At least I think I can," Marcy tells herself when she needs to confront a bat in her very own bunk five (*Bat*, 119). Life is scary, Danziger seems to murmur to her readers (and to herself?), but you will survive. Just don't take it so personally.

In the course of the novel, Marcy conquers challenges both unique and typical. She establishes independence from her family, makes new friends, has her first serious romance (in which she often takes the lead), learns how to play pinball, meets her first real-live author, and successfully faces a dreaded bat (it may be of the baseball variety, but it still permits Marcy to win her inner struggle). By summer's end she discovers that she really does have a plot and in fact, "I can hardly wait for the next chapter" (*Bat*, 150). Danziger has written that when she finished this last paragraph of *Bat*, she "felt that it summed up Marcy's life and mine."[11]

In *Bat* Marcy is still brave and forward-looking; indeed she is constantly compared to Ms. Finney for always looking on the bright side. Since *Cat*, she may have lost a bit of her edge as a wisecracker, but she remains appealing. And fortunately, she is still capable of deliciously embarrassing herself, as when her panty hose rolls down off her body just when she is picturing herself at her most glamorous. She also takes a role in one of the book's funniest scenes, the funeral ceremony for the "dearly departed bat," a tour de force of Danziger's ear for dialogue (*Bat*, 93).

Danziger's language by the time of this novel is more dependent than before on puns and "sick" jokes (including the ever-popular "What's green and hangs from trees?" "Giraffe snot" [*Bat*, 147]). Lots of them are corny and gross, but most grownups would have to admit that the humor is right for young teenagers who are just learning how to play with words.

Critical reception was mixed. Natalie Babbitt, writing in the *New York Times Book Review*, accused Danziger of oversimplification: "You of the new generation, she seems to be saying, will be fine folk someday, unlike the poor saps from whom you sprang." Such one-sided attitudes, Babbitt felt, have the effect of "romanticizing the distortions that complicate the healing of family rifts."[12] *School Library Journal* took *Bat* less seriously, acknowledging that Danziger had "skillfully balanced her insight into the daily trauma of the young adult years with liberal doses of humor. . . . The easy-to-read style will attract numerous reluctant readers and the book is sure to be extremely popular."[13] The book was "written with vigor and humor," agreed the *Bulletin of the Center for Children's Books*: "Not unusual in theme, this is unusually well done" with "depth in the relationships and characterizations" making the book unformulaic.[14]

As for Danziger, she recalls that *Bat* was "fun, easy to write in some ways." Her own summer camp experiences, however, are not the fondest of her memories. She recalls one summer when her mother showed up, brother in tow, to replace the camp nurse who had left.

This was the first book she wrote as a full-time writer, which was "a little scary, to know I wasn't going back to teaching." She was having anxiety attacks: "No paycheck every two weeks; what if I get addicted to the quiz shows on television? . . . Will I meet my deadline? When will *Kirkus Reviews* learn to love me?"[15] (The answer to that was "not imminently": Of *Bat*, *Kirkus* said it provided "pop-psychology profiles instead of imagined characters and shallow with-it attitudes instead of sincere probing."[16])

In an article written during the course of writing *Bat*, Danziger defends her change of career:

> I write of survival, the most basic of needs. . . . Most people's lives don't make newspaper headlines. But each person has the need to know who she or he is and what part she or he will play in his or her own universe. . . . I wished when growing up that there were more books that would help me to realize that I was

not alone, that there were others with some of my feelings and needs. But not many books of that time answered my wish.[17]

Bat, then, may represent Danziger's effort to write to the child she once was, to soothe and comfort. She wrote the book during her first summer in Woodstock, renting a friend's house, and it is no wonder Marcy too falls in love with the charming, arty community, just eight miles from the book's camp. Just entering Woodstock makes Marcy "want to hug everyone in the world" (*Bat*, 81).

Trite? New Age? Perhaps, especially to a jaded adult who has lost touch with what it is like to have these feelings for the first time. But, to take another perspective, it is a refreshing and healthy long way from the pitiful, deeply burrowed self Marcy Lewis started out with in *The Cat Ate My Gymsuit*.

4. A Way with Titles

The Pistachio Prescription (1978)

"This is a novel," wrote Selma G. Lanes of *The Pistachio Prescription* in the *New York Times Book Review*, "no thoughtful 9-to 13-year-old should let parents see. They may not survive the instant ego deflation of viewing themselves through adolescent eyes."[1]

Danziger's second novel is hard on parents—and teachers, siblings, friends, and its protagonist. Thirteen-year-old Cassandra (Cassie) Stephens just may not survive her own adolescence. Feeling powerless and persecuted, she is convinced that she is unique: "I'm going to explode, the first teenage bomb in captivity" (*Pistachio*, 14).

Like Marcy Lewis, Cassie is a living inferiority complex. Unlike her, Cassie has some interesting physical symptoms to go with it. She is always upset and nervous; a hypochondriac (with imaginary problems ranging from cramps to brain tumors); an asthmatic whose wheezing interferes more and more with her life ("I'm going to choke on the gunk in my lungs" [*Pistachio*, 34]—a problem that has also plagued the author); cursed with a TB ("Tiny Bladder"); and hooked on pistachios.

It is never spelled out that she compulsively indulges orally in anything other than these red, meaty nuts (though the book's last line mentions Twinkies, presumably as a joke), or that she equates all food with comfort. But the pistachios—offbeat enough in themselves—do seem to stand for a more self-destructive

addiction. Until she realizes, by the novel's end, that oral gratification does not solve anything, Cassie thinks of her pistachios as
a "prescription" for life's ills.

For most of the novel, it is hard to focus on just what Cassie's
ills might consist of. Her mother indulges her with shopping
sprees at Bloomingdale's (though she always manages to buy
more for herself than her daughter), and her father is kind and
loving, capable of genuine tears, if always away playing golf. Her
older sister, nasty at first, mellows and turns into a good friend.
Her younger brother worships her. Her best friend Vicki is cute,
popular, and wise. Everyone talks about Cassie's own good looks,
and though she thinks of herself as a "plain nobody," all she can
think of to wish for is a "smaller nose, less freckles, tinier ear
lobes" (*Pistachio*, 60). A dashing new boy moves to town and
immediately picks Cassie as his girlfriend. The school principal,
Mr. Zimmerman, thinks she is a great kid. She is a Leo and a
leader. She is good in art and plans to be an artist. And she is so
popular that her circle of friends picks her to run for "freshper-
son" class president, and she wins handily.

In many ways Cassie Stephens lives a fantasy teen's life. Yet
she wallows, for page after page, chapter after chapter, in self-
doubt and anguish. One day it is her manipulative mother, who
invades her privacy, forces her own taste on her, and seems
responsible for most of the fighting that goes on in the Stephens
household. Another day it is school, with her odious homeroom
teacher Mr. Stoddard (who usurps the role of the monster/father
in this book), and all the rules and regulations that make young
people feel powerless. Then it is her looks, on the day she decides
to tweeze her eyebrows—and is forced to don huge sunglasses
until they grow back in. Her boyfriend says one cross word to
her, and by the next paragraph she is convinced the relationship
is over and "I'm basically a loser" (*Pistachio*, 94). The times
when her parents fight are the most upsetting, inducing visions
in Cassie of becoming Lizzie Borden with her axe.

Cassie's mother, not portrayed as otherwise astute, has one of
the best lines in the book: "You are one of the most melodramatic
children I've ever seen" (*Pistachio*, 65). Teen readers, on the

other hand, are more likely to pick up on Vicki's perspective. A budding psychologist and feminist, she calls Cassie a victim of psychological child abuse. Cassie "internalizes" criticism (like "ugly" and "worthless") and allows her family to define her instead of defining herself. Her parents, far from being good role models, have "convinced you that no one's going to care about you but them" and have failed to give her "survival skills" (*Pistachio*, 95). On top of all that, she is a victim of the media's conspiracy to make all women conform to the same narrow image.

Perhaps Vicki is right, or perhaps it is just Cassie's fate to live out the legacy of her name—the character from Greek mythology whose curse it was to "speak the truth and be thought insane." Going crazy is her frequent fear ("Maybe they make straightjackets in prewashed denim" [*Pistachio*, 3]). In any case, unlike most Danziger characters, Cassie fails to keep totally buoyed by her humor. She might remember the time in fifth grade when her underpants fell down while she was at the blackboard, but now it is just a fear (that the same thing will happen when she gives her election speech), and not amusing. The tweezers incident is potentially hilarious, but Cassie sees only the tragic. Of present-day happenings, her refrain is "I'm never going to be calm enough to think this is funny" (*Pistachio*, 63).

On the day Cassie wins the election, she finds out that her parents are getting divorced. This hits her like a bombshell, even though she has been constantly aware of the "World War III" in her home. The last four chapters come into sharper focus, cramming in various tribulations experienced by children of divorce (blaming oneself, anger, visitation, parental dating, and feeling different), giving Cassie a whole new set of woes to survive. But survive she does, giving up pistachios in the process, and absorbing the meaning of the Albert Camus epigraph that begins the book: "In the midst of winter, I finally learned that there was in me an invincible summer."[2]

It is not always easy to tell what *Pistachio* is about. The author herself has described it as a book about "families that can't make it as a unit, hypochondria, addiction to pistachio nuts, and being able to accept yourself as a winner."[3] But because of Cassie's witty, self-deprecating voice throughout, the book sustains a certain unity. It is "really an extended monologue," according to the *New York Times Book Review*, "with lots of snappy one-liners, some good, some not."[4] *Booklist* called the book "funny, well-characterized (including a sympathetic school principal!), and loaded with popular appeal for the contemporary junior high set."[5] Only *Kirkus Reviews* dissented, using words like "glib" and "inauthentic." The reviewer admitted that the book was "not improbable" but still called it "shallow—a synthetic slice of 'typical teenage' life."[6]

In contrast to the Marcy (and Martin) Lewis books, in *Pistachio* it is the mother who is most responsible for the heroine's angst. She likes Cassie most when she is ill, offers fashion advice like "You need a waist to wear that" (*Pistachio*, 16), teases Cassie about her love life, and worries aloud that Cassie's too sickly to be class president. Far from supplying the high moral guidance we hope for from fictional parents when their marriages dissolve, she proposes this: "I'm sorry you're unhappy, but live with it" (*Pistachio*, 145).

Danziger tries to give the mother a motivation early on: Cassie's grandmother had multiple sclerosis, and her mother used up her youth taking care of her. But mostly she seems abusive, uncaring, or at best merely selfish.

Danziger says that at the time she was writing *Pistachio*, she "was dealing with anger at my mother, which I'm only now working out." She perceived her mother as saying hurtful or negative things, as when, for example, she told her mother she had won a young reader's award for *Cat* and was flying to Hawaii to get it. Her mother's only response was to say, "I'll pray that the plane doesn't go down."

Unlike her father, her mother was social, and she liked people and doing things. But Danziger viewed her mother as always worrying what others thought: "A major consideration in her life was that people thought well of her—as a nice, good person." This caused her to seem like "a wimp, someone who gave in easily."

Danziger saw another side to her. After having few friends when young, for example, "I fell in with a nice crowd in high school—readers, I could do my own thing, didn't have to drink. My mother said, 'Why are those girls so friendly with you? They're so pretty and popular—do they want you around for contrast?'" That she still can recall remarks like this more than thirty years later shows Danziger took them hard. She was well aware that she "was an odd little kid who didn't dress or act like anyone else. My mother used to say when I left the house, 'Do people *dress* like that?' Until one day she said, 'I get it—you dress a certain way and then in a few years *everyone* dresses like that.'" Such comments made Danziger feel that her growing up had an "inappropriate competitiveness" to it.

Danziger's brother has complained to her that their mother was always taking her shopping—to which Danziger says, "You don't understand. Shopping with me meant going to the dress department where she could buy clothes." Though she now feels that the mother in *Pistachio* "wasn't fully realized," Danziger was clearly working through some of her own feelings at the time of its writing. The book is dedicated, however, to her mother, her father—and her therapist.

Pistachio was for Danziger her biggest struggle as a writer. The circumstances under which she was writing were unfavorable, but also: "No one told me about 'second-book block.' I was brought up to be a failure, told I was not going to amount to anything. Here was this book [*Cat*], it was selling well, my fantasy come true. What if I've fooled them and have nothing left to say?" Her biggest worry was a traditional new writer's fear, that "I'm not as talented as people think, a one-book author." But her difficulties were also technical: "I didn't know these people as well, which made this hard to write."

Symptomatic of her hardship was her inability to come up with a title—a rare problem for her. Along with other trademarks (like shoes and puns—"sometimes I find myself going to sleep thinking of puns"[7]), Danziger is distinguished for unique, pithy titles that grab young adults' attention. Sometimes they come to her at the last minute, and sometimes they are on her mind for years, long before she has a plot to go with them. But all of her titles are hers—except for *The Pistachio Prescription*: "It was my hardest book to write in every way and I couldn't think of a title for it." The catchiness of this one is thanks to her publisher.

Can You Sue Your Parents for Malpractice? (1979)

The title of Danziger's third novel, on the other hand, was all hers. It has become one of her most famous (indeed, notorious): "I had the line 'can you sue your parents for malpractice?' in my head for years," she says. "It was something I wanted to do with my parents—I often threatened them with it."

The parents of Lauren Allen (named for Woody) are direct descendants of Marcy Lewis's parents: the tyrant father and the unliberated mother. *Can You Sue Your Parents for Malpractice?* is almost a sequel to *Cat*, with merely the names of the characters changed and two sisters added. One sister is a ten-year-old comedian-in-training who provides the excuse for dozens of dumb jokes throughout. The other sister, having moved in with her boyfriend, is banned from communicating with the family by their mean father—a scene never shown, as Lauren does not witness it. Like Marcy, this self-deprecating but quick-witted heroine struggles with an unhappy home life in suburban New Jersey, but she no longer takes things so personally and has gathered enough confidence now to be actively dating—and in one sense *Can You Sue Your Parents for Malpractice?* is a very sweet romance.

The "big tragedy" in Lauren's life is that her boyfriend Bobby has dumped her for a girl whose mottos are "Lust Is a Must" and "Chaste Makes Waste." While Lauren nurses her wounds by burying herself in her new class on "Law for Children and Young People" (she wants to be a lawyer), she is ripe for a romance with Zack, the nice new guy from California with the great cheekbones (a twosome set up, in part, by the sympathetic local librarian). Unfortunately, he is an eighth-grader, which subjects Lauren to a "living death" of taunts from her fellow ninth-graders. The crisis comes when she has to choose between putting up with the grief and dating someone she really likes, or returning to her prestigious but conceited and superficial former boyfriend, who wants her back after all. By this point, however, she has gotten her ears pierced and acquired a pair of "independence earrings"—a symbol of her new autonomy and her ability to make the right decisions for herself.

Told almost totally in dialogue (or else Lauren's conversations with herself), *Can You Sue Your Parents for Malpractice?* is a fast read. Teens cannot help but respond to a girl with "turd-brown curls that can't be controlled,"[8] who has some real problems but learns to alter her response to them. Scenes of dissecting frogs, pierced-ear infections, being alone with a boy in his room, fighting with one's best friend, and even household chores ("When I was born, they got a free servant" [*Malpractice*, 67]) are all minor comic disasters that spice up the angst.

Malpractice spotlights a theme that sneaks in the back door of almost every other Danziger book—the legal rights of children: "It's absolutely disgusting being fourteen. You've got no rights whatsoever. Your parents get to make all the decisions" (*Malpractice*, 12). The whole reason Lauren wants to study law is "to see that kids get an even break" (*Malpractice*, 21). But she is only half-serious about suing her parents, or maybe she realizes early on that the title question is catchy but impractical. For her class, rather than investigating this, she and Zack do a report on child abuse (his father is so physically violent that he has lost the legal right to see Zack).

By the end of the book, the question no longer even looms that large. She makes a major decision (on Bobby versus Zack) all by herself, using her own needs as guidelines—and at last a Danziger heroine is ready to take full responsibility for her own behavior. Lauren takes a giant leap forward in awareness: "Maybe suing my parents for malpractice isn't as important as making sure that I don't do malpractice on myself" (*Malpractice*, 141).

At the beginning of the book, Lauren wants to be anesthetized— "I wish there were a novocaine to numb my heart" (*Malpractice*,

24)—and she cares desperately what other people think. She blames her parents right up to the next-to-last chapter: "Why couldn't my parents have raised me to be sure of myself and to know what to do?" (*Malpractice*, 134). But by the end she knows she can face the rest of her life alert, with hope, and on her own. Instead of surviving merely through humor, Lauren learns from her older and wiser sister that "a person can survive if she does what's right for herself in spite of what others think" (*Malpractice*, 119).

This is a big, big victory, which most teen readers will cheer. They, too, can think of themselves as determining their own destiny—not an easy thing to even contemplate when you are a teen. This is one of Danziger's most empowering messages, cleverly disguised in a first-person, present-tense series of wisecracks.

Lauren's father is cruel—he doles out verbal abuse with her allowance every Saturday, makes fun of almost every move of his wife's, kicks his eldest daughter out of the house, and mystifies and terrifies his middle daughter: "I wonder what kind of man acts that way" (*Malpractice*, 75). Some days she talks back to him; some days she tries hard to please ("I practically do everything but roll over and play dead" [*Malpractice*, 104]). But it all sounds familiar: "I hate him" (*Malpractice*, 89).

By the novel's end—mirabile dictu—the father has not improved. Realizing that is another part of Lauren's hard-won wisdom: "My life's not going to drastically change. It hardly ever does when you're a kid. My parents certainly aren't going to change that much" (*Malpractice*, 141). Until she is free to live on her own, coping with her father means modifying the way *she* reacts to him—she has no hope of actually changing *him*.

Referring to the father, Danziger points out, "There's no pretty little package to wrap up. In reality, some people don't change. This book doesn't end happily ever after, and I think that's one of the things kids respond to—it doesn't lie. It's not *un*hopeful, because Lauren is a real survivor—it's not saying the world is a terrible place. The message is that it ain't always good—you have to work at it, and you may get damaged."

Lauren's father is, of course, modeled after Danziger's perception of her own father: "My brother had a different childhood," she stresses—"he loved my father very much." And her own feelings have eased, though the effects linger: "I finally *not* hated my father, but it's infected my writing and infringed on relationships, and I've had to learn not to expect that from other men." She has received some complaints about these harsh portraits over the years: "A lot of fathers are upset by the ones in my books because they think they're unredeemed. But I point out that the fathers in some of my later books are wonderful, so there's a balance. It just took a long time for me to achieve that, it took knowing other men." With *Malpractice* in particular, Danziger says, "Some (but not all) men don't like that book at all. But a lot of women (and some men) have said to me: 'That's my father—you have my father.'"

Malpractice has aroused other types of complaints as well. Except for a few minor problems (the word "bullshit" in *There's a Bat in Bunk Five*, reaction to the interracial relationship in *The Divorce Express*), Danziger has not had to deal with a lot of censorship—"I'm amazed, I'm *appalled*," she says, feigning disappointment. She recalls how John Ciardi was once put on a list of subversive speakers for colleges, and how his kids were so proud of him. *The Cat Ate My Gymsuit* occasionally runs into trouble (over the Pledge of Allegiance flap), but it is *Can You Sue Your Parents for Malpractice?* that wins the prize for the Paula Danziger book most often banned: "For the title, not by people who've actually read it, of course. Some people are afraid their kids are actually going to do it."

While certain parents may find the title lurid and disrespectful, Danziger defends it as "honest, very honest," and of course the book really does not deal with the question, much less answer it, at all. In any case, Danziger keeps certain priorities in mind: "I write books for kids, not administrators. I watch kids in bookstores—a *lot*—to see what they pick out for themselves. . . . You think Beverly Cleary or Judy Blume ever gave a thought to 'what'll sell'?"[9] Danziger writes to tell the truth and believes that "if your priority is to offend as few people as possible," you are doing a disservice to your readers, not to mention yourself as a writer.[10] With this attitude, it is amazing she has not had more problems with censorship.

Most reviewers saw eye-to-eye. "Teen readers will empathize with the heroine's problems," praised *School Library Journal*. "This novel is as much fun as Danziger's *The Cat Ate My Gymsuit*."[11] *Booklist* drew another comparison: "[Lauren's] relationships with her sisters are nicely drawn and this features the same funny, easily digested dialogue as the author's *The Pistachio Prescription*."[12] The *Journal of Reading* admired the author's "skillful balance between humor and pathos."[13]

Jane Langton, writing in the *New York Times Book Review*, was a dissenter, mocking the book for its "atmosphere[, which is] close and sweaty and mildly titillating. . . . The world of early adolescence is certainly hot and perspiring and scruffy. Open the window, somebody." As much as she found the book too narrowly focused, however, she also calls it "clever and funny" and could easily imagine all the readers that "will giggle and pass it from hand to hand"—an enviable thing to happen to an author.[14]

Danziger recalls this book as being "so much fun to write. I had gone back to college, then back to teaching junior high. This was the job interview where I put my leg up on the desk. The interviewer said, 'Am I hiring a wacko?' I said, 'Yes,' and he said, 'I just wanted to make sure.'"

Danziger had "wonderful kids" in her classes that year—all of whom are listed in the dedication to *Malpractice*. "I let them call me Paula when no one was looking, and they would tell me all their new jokes. They helped me a lot—they read the book as I was doing it, and they learned something about writing. I'd talk about how hard the book was to write, and then they'd see it. I'd come in and say, 'Guess what Lauren did today.' They'd say, 'You're writing the book—why are you surprised?'" But Danziger always *is* surprised as she is writing. Characters, especially, are always changing—these are not books written according to a formula.

In the next two books, Danziger went on to change her locale, her male parental characters—and many of her themes.

5. Children of Divorce

The Divorce Express (1984)

By the time Danziger was writing her fifth novel, the first four had sold more than two million copies in hardcover and paperback. At one point she was selling 150,000 copies of her books *a month*.[1] All four were on the "Children's Choices" list of the International Reading Association—Children's Book Council. She had received honors like being named the Multiple Sclerosis Read-a-thon Author of the Year for 1982 and 1983.

She was thus in an excellent position to publicize a subject that was just starting to get talked about: divorce from a child's point of view. When Danziger was growing up, "divorce was something to read about in movie magazines. My friends and I had parents who had been married only once. Today things have changed. Divorce is no longer a rarity."[2]

There were lots of new questions here. Are kids as resilient as we like to think they are? What do they actually experience? What are the negatives—and are there any positives? Does it leave scars, or do kids bounce back? What hurts the most? What things help? And Danziger's forte: how could you survive it?

Of *The Divorce Express* and its sequel, *It's an Aardvark-Eat-Turtle World*, Danziger says, "People always ask about these books because I've never been married. But I'd dated divorced men, some of my friends were children of divorce, and I'd been a teacher and been watching." Around this time, she was taking a course in TV writing and wrote a pilot show about a shared custody situation.

Nothing ever came of it. "I'm glad—TV people don't respect writers the way book editors do," Danziger says. But she knew this was a topic she wanted to write about.

When others question her about divorce in her own personal experience, Danziger always explains: "The easy answer is that writers don't have to deal with autobiographical experience to tell a good honest story. The real answer is that I'm not writing simply about divorce, but about people."[3]

She found a way to begin peopling and personalizing her new story on the day "a friend of mine who owns a store in Woodstock came in and said, 'I just put my kid on the Divorce Express.' I said, 'What?'" And she learned about a bus that left Woodstock every Friday for New York City and came back Sunday night, its nickname deriving from kids who went back and forth between divorced parents. It turned out that someone Danziger had hired to help with fan mail was one of the first to ride on it, and Danziger credits her with much inspiration.

The first sentence of *The Divorce Express* is almost as well known but not quite so assaultive as the "I hate my father" of *Cat*: "Rearrange the letters in the word PARENTS and you get the word ENTRAPS."[4] This fourteen-year-old wordplayer has problems ("It's not fair" comes three sentences later), but she is also refreshingly mellow. Danziger has moved so far from autobiography that she has her heroine gushing early on: "I love you too. I think you're wonderful" (*Divorce*, 14)—*to her father* (he has obligingly released a raccoon from another sort of trap).

Phoebe Brooks (named for comedian Mel, and for Holden Caulfield's little sister in *The Catcher in the Rye*) is involved in a confusing joint custody arrangement in which she has had next to no say. Her parents, not being child psychology experts, have not handled this circumstance particularly well, and Phoebe has already done a lot of "acting out." Her loudest cry for help, the time she Krazy-Glues everything she can in her New York school, gets a week's suspension, a large bill to pay off, and a more sane living arrangement. The school's guidance counselor points out that "maybe I just wanted something in my life to stay in one place" (*Divorce*, 4), and Phoebe goes off to live with her father in Woodstock, seeing her mother in New York City only on weekends.

As transportation, Phoebe uses the Divorce Express, a bus that becomes a metaphor for the roller coaster ride through the land of contemporary divorce. Danziger uses plenty of specific details to illustrate Phoebe's life: two homes, two lifestyles; two sets of friends, clothes—and chores; trying to get homework done while shuttling around; a boyfriend lost in one city because she was not around to sustain the relationship; worry over keeping the new boyfriend. The logistics of a dual life can be wearying. No wonder Phoebe sometimes feels isolated, different, and confused—"as if my heart is on a yo-yo" (*Divorce*, 36). Part of her angst is just normal adolescence, as Danziger spells out in her epigraph from John Ciardi: "You don't have to suffer to be a poet. Adolescence is enough suffering for anyone."

Much of it is divorce-related, though, and Danziger does a masterful job in bringing to life some real emotional hardships children of divorce have to get through: Watching a once-loving relationship disintegrate before your eyes, and having the two people you most love not being able to stand each other. Having a parent emotionally or physically unavailable to you just when you need one, as when Phoebe wants some immediate cooking guidance from her long-distance mother. Protecting a parent's feelings, which Phoebe does a lot though she realizes it is above and beyond the call of duty for a child. Keeping on a schedule with a parent, with no time just to "hang out." Listening to them criticize each other and find fault, without regard for your feelings.

The problems never cease: Watching as your parents start to date people you cannot stand. Having to share them and compete for their attention. Picturing them sleeping with new people. Being confused when they sleep with each other even after the divorce. Coping with the entrances and exits of potential stepmothers and stepfathers in your life, people who may someday have very real power over you. Having parents use you as a message-bearing go-between, even about strictly parental matters like child support payments. Seeing your parents as people and realizing you may not like them much. Dealing with money as a constant battleground and worry, when most kids do not have to think about it. Doubting *you* will ever have a marriage that works.

As for the positives, they are hard-won strengths: Phoebe finds that kids who live through divorces become better at handling other problems, because they have already had to solve so many. When you have survived "rough stuff," you develop a sense of perspective about the smaller stuff. You especially grow up fast when you have to act the grown-up to your parents, helping with their loneliness and unhappiness. You learn that you have to control your own life, because you certainly cannot control your parents' ups and downs. Independence comes faster when you realize you cannot depend on your parents for everything anymore. You get two sets of presents—and sometimes even more, from parents working out their guilt at their transgressions. And you definitely get to travel a lot more—a broadening of your horizons.

Phoebe Brooks is not making new friends in Woodstock, just trying to blend into the background at Joyce Kilmer High School, until the day she throws caution to the wind and dons her beaded American Indian earrings and ties a scarf around her head. This expression of individuality pays off immediately when she attracts the attention of Rosie Wilson, another flashy dresser and a kindred soul: "I like looking different," she says—daring language for a teen (*Divorce*, 34). Phoebe puts her foot in her mouth by asking about Rosie's tan, and her new friend reveals that she is the child of an interracial marriage that crumbled when she was three. A Divorce Express regular, she is the perfect person to help Phoebe cope—and also to play with. After buying a unicorn shirt together (symbolizing an imaginary better life for both), they become such close friends that they think of themselves as sisters.

Danziger throws in an interesting curve ball when she has Phoebe's father Jim and Rosie's mother Mindy start dating. Are the girls going to become sisters after all? A more serious crisis comes when Phoebe's mother decides to marry Duane ("the Drip"), a man with a long list of faults. (At least Phoebe *likes*

Mindy.) Her father comes to her rescue and helps her realize that her attitude will make a difference now and in the future: "I have to learn how to handle this new situation so that it works out well for me . . . as well as it can without it being what I really want" (*Divorce*, 143).

So she elects *not* to send that sympathy card to her mother, but to attend the wedding as she knows she should. At the novel's end she does not even feel entrapped anymore, and she is learning to create her own space in the world. She now looks outward and, in a nice unifying twist, says, "If you take the letters in the word DIVORCES and rearrange them, they spell DISCOVER" (*Divorce*, 148). She plans to keep on riding the Divorce Express, and it is not at all clear that she is talking about the bus.

Despite the seriousness of the topics, *Divorce* is not a heavy book. Danziger lightens the load with a frothy subplot that continues the social protest theme more prominent in her other books: children are not powerless—they have rights. Here it is the inedible cafeteria lunches that unite the school in revulsion. Phoebe already has had experience with this at her previous school. When students organize their protest at Joyce Kilmer High she hears about the nonviolent philosophies of Thoreau, Gandhi, and Martin Luther King Jr. Though she gets outvoted on the group's name—KRAPS, for Kilmerites Rebel Against Poor Sustenance—she is able to take a lead role in the protest, especially when it comes to wordplay like anagrams and parodies. She spearheads the comic, ultimately victorious struggle to improve the quality of school food, a subject dear to almost any teenager's heart.

Comedy crops up elsewhere, as when Phoebe meets her future boyfriend Dave ("smart, funny, and very cute" [*Divorce*, 63]) by accidentally swinging her knapsack into his head. And Phoebe knows how to giggle: "The only badge I hope that Dave earned was in lifesaving—specializing in mouth-to-mouth resuscitation" (*Divorce*, 107). *Divorce* is also in part a love song to Woodstock, portrayed as an artistic haven from the real world; the novel is dedicated "to the town and people of Woodstock" (as well as to twenty-six people in particular).

Phoebe has made progress with the self-image problem plaguing earlier Danziger protagonists. She thinks she looks okay—not glamorous, but it is not "necessary to go out into the world covered by a yard-size Hefty garbage bag either" (*Divorce*, 105). She flirts easily with boys, and the course of true love with Dave runs smooth.

What about fathers? Jim in *Divorce* is one of the fathers Danziger thinks of as balancing out her earlier unredeemable dads. "What's changed in my life is the anger, it's gone now, toward fathers," she says. Phoebe's father is a music-loving painter, a vegetarian and pacifist, and a man who communicates so openly with Phoebe that she sometimes wishes he would stop. He calls her "honey," takes her to concerts, and is openly affectionate and cooperative—a dream dad except that he is still "getting his act together" regarding relationships. Danziger can see now that "not until the writing of *Divorce* did I stop being angry at fathers."

Though nitpicking that the treatment of divorce was "timely rather than profound," *Horn Book* praised the work: "The author has a sympathetic ear for the ups and downs of her characters and a quick ear for adolescent conversation."[5] *Growing Point* pinpointed the reason for the novel's continued popularity: "Mercifully avoiding the inspissated gloom and wearisome heart-searching of so many novels on this highly topical subject, *The Divorce Express* makes its point in an agreeably relaxed and shrewd manner."[6] *Booklist* concurred that "Danziger's light style laced with humor will continue to attract readers."[7]

The *Bulletin of the Center for Children's Books* argued that *Divorce* was not "structurally strong or innovative," but acknowledged its "great vitality and humor."[8] And the *New York Times Book Review*, while wondering if "the breezy, fast-paced, often humorous first-person narrative" and "simplistic" characterizations did not "muffle" the traumatic impact of divorce, also called the book "an undeniable 'good read.'"[9]

Criticism aside, the fact that Danziger went through numerous revisions in order to *make* the book a good read in turn makes young adults eager to read it—in all the years since it has been published. She notes that when she started the book, "There were not a lot of parents making [shared custody] arrangements. Now there are many more."[10] Divorce and all its implications is a much wider field these days, and *Divorce* is one book for which the audience does not seem likely, statistically, to shrink.

It's an Aardvark-Eat-Turtle World (1985)

One of the reviews of which Danziger is most proud came from one of her favorite writers. Anne Tyler, in the *Washington Post*, writes: "Paula Danziger is probably best known for *The Cat Ate My Gymsuit*, but I found *It's an Aardvark-Eat-Turtle World* superior, particularly in its avoidance of the black-and-white, good-guy-bad-guy aspects of some of her earlier books." Tyler praises the book for presenting divorce issues "realistically and sympathetically": "As an experienced teacher and counselor, she knows the intricacies of contemporary adolescent life, and she puts her knowledge to good use in this story."[11]

The sequel to *Divorce* came about because Danziger found she genuinely cared about these characters: "It was hard for me to let go of this book even when I knew it had reached its logical ending."[12] And there were still some issues left untreated, such as, What happens when families blend?

Danziger foreshadowed her own sequel in the earlier book, when she has Rosie comment on novels for young adults about divorce: "They're mostly for the kids who are just starting it. There should be one about a kid who's lived with it for a long time" (*Divorce*, 57). A kid like Rosie, for example, who has lived with divorce for eleven years and does not remember what a "real" family is like.

With *It's an Aardvark-Eat-Turtle World*, Danziger switches narrators and tells the story from Rosie's point of view. She started out writing the novel as being narrated by Phoebe again but eventually realized that the book—because of Phoebe's inability, after all, to handle her mother's remarriage—was sounding "so *angry*." A friend asked her who she really liked in the story, and "it became clear that Rosie had to tell the second story. She tries to live with creativity and flair, she's passionate—even her clothes were something I responded to."[13] It was a case of a character developing and taking over.

The inspiration for Rosie's comment about divorce books came from kids who were helping with Danziger's fan mail: "One day one of them said, 'There are all these books helping kids through a divorce—what about those of us who have lived with it our entire lives?' That helped me focus." Listening has always been the key to Danziger's themes and insights, plus "having to be creative on top of it." She can be sitting in a restaurant eating breakfast, and someone at the next table could be doing something imaginative, and she will think, "I could use that in a book . . . but I'll carry it on to something else. You don't just put something in a book once, you bring it back again."

One of the elements that gets repeated in *It's an Aardvark-Eat-Turtle World* is the title, one of Danziger's more unusual. The people Rosie baby-sits for (she refers to her charge privately as "Little Nerdlet") have a dog, Aardvark, who is in the habit of eating the arrivals from the pet-of-the-month club, including the recently arrived (and departed) turtle. Her cynical city father is always telling Rosie "it's a dog-eat-dog world," but Rosie puts her comic twist on life: "It's an aardvark-eat-turtle world."[14]

By the end of the novel, Rosie does not even believe that anymore. Instead: "It's a world where families and friendships change and grow. It sure takes a lot of work, but it's worth it" (*Aardvark*, 132). Rosie does not reach this wisdom, of course, without a struggle. In the beginning, she spells out exactly what she needs: "What I really want more than anything is to be part of a family, all living happily under one roof" (*Aardvark*, 1). As events evolve, she gets her heart's desire—for exactly one day.

She and her writer/waitress mother, Mindy Kovacs (named after comedian Ernie), have been pals for so many years, on a first-name basis ever since Rosie decided so in kindergarten. Now they are moving in with Phoebe and her father Jim. They all hold hands and hope and pray that the new arrangement works, but there is no actual marriage ceremony, making it only an unofficial stepfamily. Rosie is so anxious for the new family to succeed that she gives up her cat and dog (because of Jim's allergies) and having her own room—she and messy Phoebe will now share.

Crisis looms (a bit unbelievably) on the very first day, when Mindy takes it upon herself to chastise Phoebe for "making out" with her boyfriend Dave in front of the whole neighborhood. Phoebe "snarls," "stares her down," "stamps her foot," "backs off"—in short, completely overreacts (*Aardvark*, 32). World War III is on, and unfortunately for Rosie and her heart's desire, it lasts throughout the book.

Seeing Phoebe through Rosie's eyes, we view her differently and more critically: she is childish, self-involved, manipulative around boys, not as good at making new friends as we thought, much more of a shopaholic than she ever told us, and not handling her changing situation nearly as well as we would have hoped from her brave stance in the earlier book. Her mother is married to a creep (no redeeming qualities for Duane are ever apparent), and so Phoebe has lost her confidante. Her father has moved in with a woman who immediately bosses her around, and so Phoebe has lost her pal. On top of everything else, when Phoebe brings Rosie along on a trip to Toronto, she "loses" Rosie to a new flame, Jason ("nice, cute, and punny" [*Aardvark*, 77]). The only one to stick with her is Dave, and for a while he is her only reason for being in Woodstock.

Everyone is furious, blaming Phoebe for sabotaging the new blended family. Rosie, with her central motivation being to have one big happy family, plays peacemaker and almost always offers the first moves. But even she admits, "It's not so easy making happily ever after work" (*Aardvark*, 49).

The tension peaks during an airport scene when all the principal characters are forced to come face-to-face and to be polite to each other. The "weird and irresponsible" Woodstockers meet the wealthy uptight New Yorkers. Subsequently, while in Toronto, Phoebe's mother pressures her to move in with her and Duane in New York, and in her turmoil and without confiding in Rosie, Phoebe succumbs. Rosie thinks an alien has taken over her former best friend's body. Suddenly she does not have to share a room anymore, and Jim is calling her "Phoebe" by mistake.

Some six weeks later, Phoebe has a (not fully explained) change of heart and wants to return to Woodstock. As long as she is "willing to make changes and to get some counseling" (*Aardvark*, 127), the others take her back. Mindy sacrifices too: having sold her first children's book, she gives up her home office (renting an office in town) so the girls can have their own rooms. And Rosie learns to accept that she still wants a family even if it does have problems.

Praise for *Aardvark* came from the *Bulletin of the Center for Children's Books*: "This has moments of sweetness to balance some tartness, an honest approach to problems, a lively and natural writing style, and strong, consistent characterization."[15] According to the *Voice of Youth Advocates*, the book's "second half didn't quite live up to the promise of the first," but "junior highs will buzz to it" regardless.[16] "Depth is sacrificed to flippancy," disagreed *School Library Journal*.[17] But in at least one respect Danziger was ahead of her time: The *Interracial Books for Children Bulletin* recommended the book as the first they had seen that "approaches the subject of interracial children and some of the problems they encounter."[18]

Several things in the book remind the reader that Rosie is half black—her excellent collection of books by African-American authors, an ugly racial incident in Toronto, and worry about her unusual looks. Danziger is sometimes asked just why she made Rosie's parents interracial. "There are interracial kids in Woodstock," she says, but more than that, "I don't think there are enough black and interracial kids in books, especially on covers. I think it's important to see black kids on covers. When they're there, it's usually because the book is about *being* black or Hispanic." Once she made this choice, Danziger found herself worrying about issues of political correctness—for example, it is Rosie's (black) father who is always behind in his child support checks.

She always comes back to her priorities, though: "Wait a minute—I'm writing about separate people and these are two people and this is their experience." As with all of her novels, "these are just kids, just people trying to get through life."

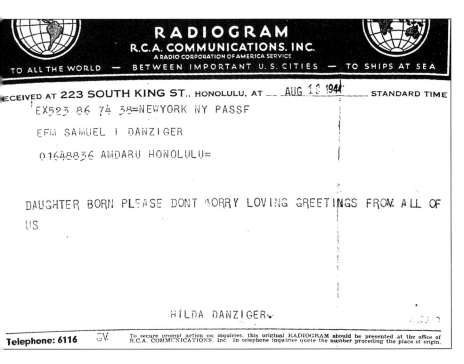

RECEIVED AT 223 SOUTH KING ST., HONOLULU, AT ___ AUG 13 1944 ___ STANDARD TIME

EX523 86 74 38=NEWYORK NY PASSF

EFM SAMUEL I DANZIGER

01648836 AMDARU HONOLULU=

DAUGHTER BORN PLEASE DONT WORRY LOVING GREETINGS FROM ALL OF US

HILDA DANZIGER.

Telephone: 6116   GV.   To secure prompt action on inquiries, this original RADIOGRAM should be presented at the office of R.C.A. COMMUNICATIONS, Inc. In telephone inquiries quote the number preceding the place of origin.

Exchange of telegrams between Paula Danziger's parents on the occasion of her birth. "DAUGHTER BORN PLEASE DON'T WORRY," wrote her mother.

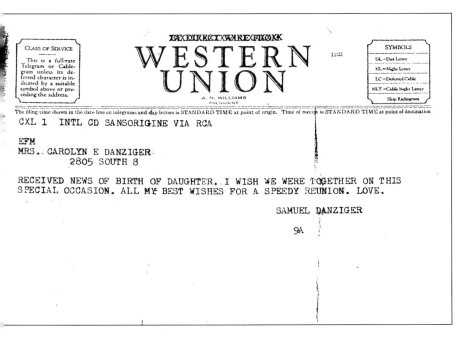

The filing time shown in the date line on telegrams and day letters is STANDARD TIME at point of origin. Time of receipt is STANDARD TIME at point of destination

CXL 1   INTL CD SANSORIGINE VIA RCA

EFM
MRS. CAROLYN E DANZIGER
2805 SOUTH 8

RECEIVED NEWS OF BIRTH OF DAUGHTER. I WISH WE WERE TOGETHER ON THIS SPECIAL OCCASION. ALL MY BEST WISHES FOR A SPEEDY REUNION. LOVE.

SAMUEL DANZIGER

9A

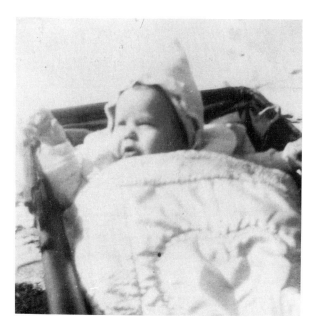

Baby Paula (above) and with her mother (right), who writes on the back of the photo, "This is the baby's method of letting us know she wants to play, I think."

Paula, age 5, getting along with her brother Barry, age 2.

Paula as toddler, swinging with her mother (left) and both parents (below).

Non-animal-loving Paula at the Bronx Zoo (above) and behind the wheel (below).

With her mother.

Future celebrity (left)
and future celebrity
with glasses (below).

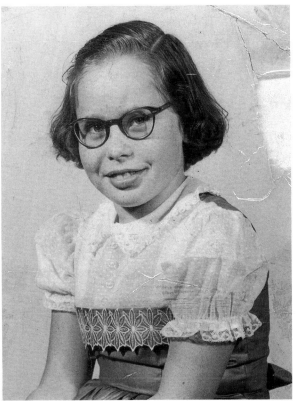

"I'm so glad they invented contact lenses" is Danziger's response to pictures of her at age 9 (top) and in the high school yearbook (bottom).

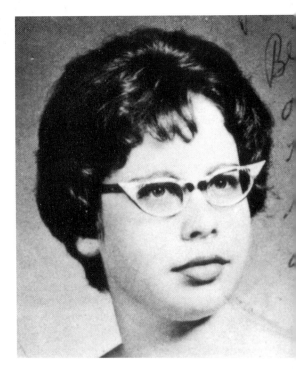

Danziger's travels while making promotional appearances have taken her from the frigidity of Alaska (upper left) to the glitter of Las Vegas (upper right) to the heights of Scotland (bottom).

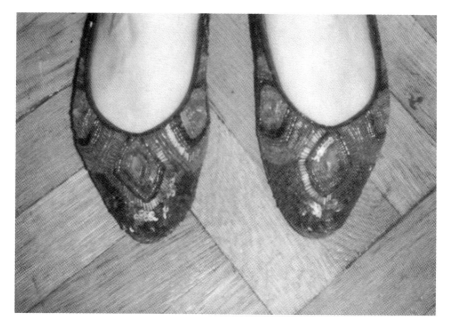

Wherever she journeys, it is preferably in a pair of sequined shoes.

Paula is going to be this many years old!

and "shoe enough" it's steppin' out time...

I ALWAYS THOUGHT SHE HAD SOLE HER REMARKS ARE SO TONGUE IN CHEEK

SHE DEFINITELY IS NOT STRAIGHT LACED AND SHE'S NO LOAFER IF SHE'D STOP SHOPPING SHE'D

BE WELL HEELED I GAVE HIM THE BOOT HE SAYS HE

LOVES ME, HE SAYS HE DOESN'T LOVE ME (THAT'S WHAT YOU GET FOR DATING FLIP FLOPS).

Date

August 6, 1994

Time

7:00 Hors d'oeuvres

8:00 Dinner

Place

Catskill Rose

Rte. 212

Mt. Tremper

New York

(shirt and shoes required)

Danziger's invitation to her fiftieth birthday party (left and above)
plays on her fetish for fancy shoes.

I, Amber Brown, am one very excited third grader. Just look at my reviews!

★"This heroine's perky first-person narrative allows readers to make her acquaintance immediately — and effortlessly. Once again, PAULA DANZIGER demonstrates her ability to connect with her audience. One hopes she has more escapades planned for Amber."—*Publishers Weekly*, starred review

"It's grand to have PAULA DANZIGER add books for younger readers to her many popular titles for the older crowd." —*Kirkus Reviews*

Great, huh? I've been practicing my signature for when I get famous... So here it is —

Amber Brown

PAULA DANZIGER'S
Amber Brown is Not a Crayon

Illus. in black and white by Tony Ross
Ages 6-9/0-399-22509-9/$12.95 ($16.95 CAN)
FREE bookmarks and press kits available

G.P. PUTNAM'S SONS
Member of The Putnam & Grosset Group
200 Madison Avenue, New York, NY 10016

Illustration © 1994 by Tony Ross
© 1994 The Putnam & Grosset Group

Coming in the Fall: THAMES DOESN'T RHYME WITH JAMES

Danziger's latest books are earning her the kind of full-page advertisements that are the envy of other writers for young people.

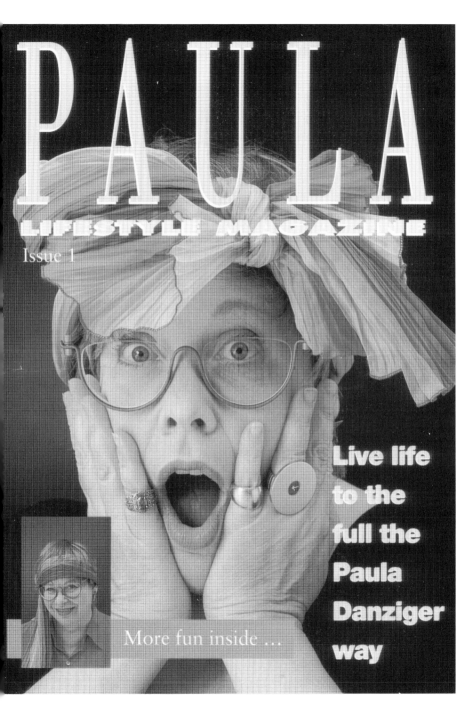

PAULA

LIFESTYLE MAGAZINE

Issue 1

Live life to the full the Paula Danziger way

More fun inside ...

The promotional efforts of Danziger's British publisher include her own periodical—the giddy *Paula Lifestyle Magazine*. "Live life to the full the Paula Danziger way!"

A DAY IN THE LIFE

First thing in the morning it's straight down to work. A writer's life is arduous and solitary.

8am

9am

Paula looks to her muse for inspiration. A 'mermaid moment'.

Paula hates clutter. Her fanmail is meticulously filed away. Along with her extensive sticker collection.

10am

11am

Paula phones her editor to catch up on booktrade gossip.

11:30am

Whilst correcting the first draft of another blockbusting megaseller the author relaxes in her sensible shoes.

12pm

Paula gasps as she realises she is late for her face-painting appointment.

The *Lifestyle Magazine* includes a blow-by-blow account of "A Day in the Life of Paula"—part tongue-in-cheek, part literal truth.

1pm

The tiger face is one of her favourites.

2pm

Paula stalks through the undergrowth. Method acting helps her develop characters...

Research gathering takes many forms. Paula takes tea at Bibendum.

3pm

Trafalgar Square fountains are perfect for removing greasepaint.

4pm

Now, where *did* I leave all those shopping bags?

4:30pm

5pm

Paula loves to relax with books...

Paula prepares for another wild party with her friends.

7.30pm

Decisions ... Decisions ...

The magazine comes to a close with Danziger's final bit of glamour—"another wild party with her friends."

6. From New York to Outer Space and Back Again

This Place Has No Atmosphere (1986)

"The light bulbs in Juna's hair flash on and off as she talks." Who is this? Where are we? Are we still in Paula Danziger territory?

In her seventh novel, presumably not overtly autobiographical, Danziger takes a wild leap into the year 2057 and spins a science fiction story for young adults. Why? "I love science fiction," she explains, "and I especially liked Asimov and Bradbury as a kid— *Illustrated Man, Dangerous Visions*. My strength is not plot, but I thought I'd try it." According to Danziger, teens are teens— "just trying to get through life"—whether they're in New York State or on the moon, trying to survive the 1990s or the 2050s.

The title of *This Place Has No Atmosphere* refers to both a physical and ironic fact about the new home for thirteen-year-old Aurora Borealis Williams (named for comedian Robin). Very much against her will, her medical superstar parents are moving to the colony on the moon for five years and taking her with them. Only 750 people live there, in an airtight bubble, and among them Aurora is sure there will not be a single boy she likes. Hers is the perennial complaint of teens around the universe: "It's so not fair."[1]

At the beginning of the novel, while still on earth, Aurora is shallow, boy-crazy, and self-involved (albeit still likable). She takes for granted the circumstances of her space-age life: Robot monitors patrol the cafeteria, doling out detention for various infractions. Juna, Aurora's best friend, has trendy hair—purple, pink, different lengths, tipped with silver, and laced with tiny light bulbs. The school runs on garbage—the latest thing in power sources—and kids take classes in ESP and building synthesizers.

Aurora's favorite hangout, the Monolith Mall, has forty blissful floors of stores and moving sidewalks. People wear "Walkperson earrings" to hear their own music and "mood clothes" that reflect in rainbow colors how they feel. Books are all on disk, and smoking cigarettes is illegal. The latest sensations are Rita Retrograde, whose releases come in holograph form, and a group called the Jackson 127 (descendants of the Jackson Five). The president is a woman, and Disney is the fifty-first state.

Much of the humor in *Atmosphere* comes from the way Danziger works in futuristic details—almost lovingly—as if to tickle the reader. Partly it is a crafty focus on what kids today would really want to know about the future, and partly it is some obvious wish fulfillment of her own.

Aurora is part of the in crowd, which is known in her school as the Turnips (because they are always "turning up" to make appearances). Whenever she is unhappy, she shops. Hanging out with her friends means she does not have to think about anything serious. The others consider her cool, for all the best superficial reasons: "My house is in the right neighborhood, a lot of kids think I'm kind of cute, and I'm in a lot of school plays" (*Atmosphere*, 4). They make fun of others, gossip, and spend lots of money and most of their time conforming. No real trouble, although Aurora did have to break up with her last boyfriend when he was frying his brain with drugs and he chose drugs over her: "I've heard that he's had to go into a drug rehab program. I'm sorry, but I really don't want to have anything to do with him anymore" (*Atmosphere*, 16).

Aurora has never gone more than a few minutes without a boyfriend; it is a family joke that her first printed words were wedding invitations. Her newest heartthrob, Matthew, ninth grade class president, makes her life complete when he asks her to the homecoming dance, called "Evening on Jupiter." He has had a crush on her since second grade, when she drew on walls instead of in coloring books. The two are soulmates who love wordplay and cannot even go out for a simple ice cream without outdoing Baskin-Robbins: "Owl pellet peach, mucous mocha, snot sundae, phlegm frappe," and so on (*Atmosphere*, 15).

"Some things don't change," Danziger points out about the difference in centuries. "Parents are still going to fight with kids in a hundred years." In *Atmosphere*, then, school lunches are still disgusting; brownies are still the best comfort food. Kids still squeeze pimples and complain about their families. Girls still get along better with their grandmothers sometimes than with their mothers. In Aurora's case, the mother-daughter relationship is weirder than ever, since her mother, a parapsychology expert, can literally read her mind—a teenager's worst nightmare.

On the day Aurora sets aside, at her sympathetic grandmother's urging, to make a real effort to get along with her mother, she finds out about the moon move. As usual with Danziger heroines, she is at first utterly powerless: "Kids have no say" (*Atmosphere*, 32). Aurora is a budding actress, with a bigger-than-usual flair for the dramatic, and devotes herself to moping. She makes superficial snap judgments about her new acquaintances on the moon—"they're 'Turndowns' instead of 'Turnips'" (*Atmosphere*, 67)—and she is lost without her former friends. She cannot prove to anyone that she used to be popular and important. In fact, she is so used to running with a group that she does not even really know who she is. It is a familiar teen syndrome.

Little by little, Aurora uncoils, developing some pioneer spirit. Among the forty-five kids on the moon, she starts finding her way. She helps a pitiful kid her age—Julie Verne—learn how to use makeup. She discovers she actually enjoys her assigned service project, which is taking care of the Eaglettes—the kids under five. She likes her older guide, tall and brainy Hal, even though he would never fit in with the Turnips. She stops worrying so much about what other people think. In fact, she is starting to see that the Turnips are cruel and, amazingly, that she is outgrowing them. She even looks out for her little sister Starr—voluntarily.

With no malls, weather, or any scenery to distract her, nor hours in the bath (to conserve water only two six-minutes showers are permitted a week), she throws herself into mounting and starring in a performance of Thorton Wilder's play, *Our Town*. It is a considerable distance from the lights of Broadway, but it is the only theater in town.

Unfortunately, Aurora fails to get the lead role she wanted, Emily, and must settle for Mrs. Gibbs. This is a terrible blow to her ego, and at first all she does is throw temper tantrums. Then her wise teacher helps her realize the central theme of *Atmosphere*, that each person is "a part of the universe"—not the center (*Atmosphere*, 130). She takes this to heart, portrays Mrs. Gibbs brilliantly, and is rewarded by realizing just how much she has grown as a person. She elects to stay on the moon, not taking the first chance she has to move back. Eventually she plans to get herself to Paris (still a goal for twenty-first-century budding bohemians), but meanwhile there are new worlds to discover: "Instead of outer space, inner space" (*Atmosphere*, 138).

Finding out that the universe does *not* revolve around you is a lesson all young adults need to tackle; some never do, or for others, like Danziger, the lesson comes later rather than sooner: "When you're that angry, it takes longer," she says about herself. In *Atmosphere* she uses a most unusual setting and time period to bring to life one of the most important learning tasks on the road to adulthood.

Now that Aurora knows, for example, how miserable it is to be the new kid, she wishes she had been kinder to new kids at her old school. But most teens seldom think of anyone but themselves in this fashion—Aurora is not unusually self-centered, she is the norm. At the novel's end, it is not clear her newest romance (with Hal) will last; she may have some more distance to go before she is a "fully developed individual," as her mother primly puts it (*Atmosphere*, 24).

Besides futuristic allusions, *Atmosphere* is laced with references to another new topic: holistic medicine, such as acupuncture (which Danziger has been using for years, for pain), chiropractics, reflexology points, biofeedback, herbs, and aloe plants (used to cure burns). Aurora's father is a holistic dentist who uses acupuncture and TENS (electrical stimulation) for pain, gemstones and colors to heal, and visualization techniques to straighten teeth. It is a frequent-dental-patient's fantasy.

Holistic medicine is of personal interest to Danziger, who is an especially strong believer in the healing power of hands: "As people we all have a quality inside ourselves that we can center and calm enough to help others. For someone whose hands go out of socket, I have discovered an incredible strength and gentleness in my hands."

In addition, as part of the research for *Atmosphere*, Danziger traveled not quite to the moon, but to NASA in Houston for help with some of the details of space flight. This being exploration for a Paula Danziger book, misadventures resulted as well, as when she got trapped on the second level of the space shuttle simulator.

School Library Journal cheered *Atmosphere* as a "mischievous spoof of a science fiction novel as well as a warm and funny saga about a teen of the future who is having severe difficulties adjusting to a family move."[2] The story has "universal" appeal, according to the *Horn Book*: "All the author's flair for teen talk, humor, and clothes is apparent in her latest romp."[3] The *Bulletin of the Center for Children's Books* found Aurora "a typical Danziger heroine—smart, with a rueful, dead-pan humor." They pinpointed a few clichés of the "paperback romance" type, but overall judged the narration and voice "smoother than they have been in Danziger's last few novels."[4]

While *Kirkus Reviews* demurred that "a Danziger book is rarely distinguished by plot, characterization or literary style," they followed in the next sentence with praise many authors of young adult books would most likely kill for: "She does hone in, unerringly, on the concerns of her audience, using a style that rat-tats out wisecracks. . . . Her audiences will not be disappointed."[5]

Remember Me to Harold Square (1987)

From the universe's first Off-Off-Off-Off-Off-Off-Off-Broadway play to "Give My Regards to Broadway"—Danziger in her next novel gives us *Remember Me to Harold Square*. The punning title comes from the George M. Cohan song, whose second line a Wisconsinite misunderstands in the book to be about a real guy named Harold—instead of *Herald* Square, the area around Macy's department store.

Fourteen-year-old Kendra Kaye (named for comedian Danny) is stuck for the summer in New York City, while her wealthier friends from her small private school go off to camps and fancy vacations. Her biggest problems are the dustballs under her bed, a nagging mother, a secret suspicion that boys are from another planet and she will never understand them—and everything else in the world.

In a metaphor that gains meaning throughout the entire novel, Kendra identifies with the fragile butterflies in her collection. It is perplexing when your body is changing almost as drastically as a caterpillar changes into a butterfly, and it creates anxiety to think about leaving the cocoon: "Just as soon as you get used to things being one way, you turn into something else—a butterfly or what books refer to as 'a young adult.'"[6]

Perhaps because Kendra is a bit older than other Danziger heroines (or because this is the author's eighth novel), she sounds a little more mature and balanced. Her rough edges have already been considerably smoothed, and she is considerate of others' feelings, kind to strangers, with even a fairly penetrating understanding of her mother and her "one sighs fits all" (*Harold*, 2) attitude. She is between boyfriends—having realized that her relationship with the last one "was not destined to be the love of the century, or even of the marking period" (*Harold*, 6)—but not desperate about it. Gone is the anger of past Danziger heroines; Kendra is merely confused, searching for enlightenment.

In a slightly contrived but fun development, Frank Lee, a cute, blond fifteen-year-old, arrives from Wisconsin to stay with the family for the summer. His parents are off to Europe and have concocted a plan with Kendra's parents to send her, her precocious ten-year-old brother Oscar, and Frank on a complicated scavenger hunt around New York. The goal is to get them to know the city inside and out, and as incentive to make sure the kids actually follow through, the prize is a trip to England for all of them—one of Kendra's biggest goals ("I can already speak the language" [*Harold*, 34]). It is the ultimate in games, sending them off on a whirlwind tour that includes a total of twenty museums and galleries, fifteen historic places, fifteen neighborhoods, eight cultural activities, and twenty-two types of ethnic food. Complete answers to the scavenger hunt questions are provided by Danziger in a fact-filled back section.

The hunt is a tactic that allows Danziger to not only keep Kendra busy and maturing, but also to sing a song of praise to New York City. Not everything is perfect here—there are roaches, poverty and homeless people, dirt and graffiti, high prices, traffic gridlock, and the need to be on guard against crime—but it is clearly, according to *Harold*, the most exciting city in the world. Famous people stroll the sidewalks, stretch limos round street corners, the cultural riches are endless, and it is never boring—Danziger brings the city to life in a way teens can relate to.

Frank turns out to have a semidark past—his parents are on the verge of divorce, his father has cancer, and he is involved in a serious relationship with an eighteen-year-old back home that his parents are trying to break up—and Kendra's very first reaction shows what a good person she is. She starts thinking of Frank as a "survivor" rather than as a prospective boyfriend, and she immediately wants to help. Of course, as soon as she learns how to be good friends with a boy (and that boys are caterpillars, too), romance rears its sexy head. Kendra and Frank end up as best friends, romantically involved—and separated (he returns to Wisconsin). But it is implied that they will meet up again in London to visit Trafalgar Square (Harold Square's English cousin), not to mention one of Kendra's favorite people, Aunt Judy. (And so they do in the sequel, *Thames Doesn't Rhyme with*

James.) Meanwhile, Kendra has fallen in love with New York City and plans a new school year in which she will treat boys like human beings.

As befits her bighearted heroine, Danziger uses this book to tackle some tough topics. Nazi persecution, for example, had been one of Danziger's worst fears as a child growing up in a Jewish family (and it was always so frustrating to never get past World War I in school). At the time she was writing *Harold*, Kurt Waldheim, whose knowledge of German war crimes was under investigation, had just been elected president of Austria. As a teacher, she had seen kids thoughtlessly doodling swastikas in notebooks, and in *Harold* she decided to talk about the Holocaust.

She uses it in two ways, one of which is to give depth and motivation to Kendra's mother. Mrs. Kaye's parents were imprisoned in a concentration camp. Though they escaped alive, they lost many relatives and their experience scarred them and the next generation. Her parents' nightmare is what causes Kendra's mother to be such a worrywart about Kendra: "They were always so worried, so afraid that something bad would happen. I grew up trying to make everything good for them, trying to be perfect" (*Harold*, 93).

Hearing about this touches Kendra deeply, as perhaps it was affecting Danziger to contemplate her own father's family history. Making it all even more real to Kendra is her visit to the Holocaust exhibit at the Jewish Museum, one of three excursions that merits a separate chapter (besides a Mets game and a tour of the set of *All My Children*, Kendra's favorite show). Kendra is so saddened and depressed by the George Segal sculpture depicting concentration camp victims that at first she can hardly speak. Then she reverts to calling her mother "Mommy," seeking adult comfort. Learning about historical horrors is disturbing enough, but even more "devastating" is thinking about all the oppression there still is in the world.

There are no snappy one-liners in this section, nor in the subsequent references to Hiroshima and Nagasaki. It is Danziger's way of enlightening teens about the chilling problems around the world, and then sympathizing with them for being the generation to inherit some enormous responsibilities.

It bothers Danziger that some people have accused her of "throwing" the Holocaust into the plot, as for example when the *Bulletin of the Center for Children's Books* wrote: "The one serious experience of a Holocaust exhibit seems forced into a glib context."[7] Says Danziger: "The Holocaust wasn't 'thrown in.' It's there because I wanted kids to know that it happened. I wanted to say, 'As long as people aren't free.' . . . I also didn't want to hit them over the head with it."

In any case, Kendra does not stay depressed; she remains light on her feet, a survivor herself. She knows, for example, that "silliness with words is one of my favorite things" (*Harold*, 40), and like any self-respecting Danziger character, she plays with them constantly. In an especially witty touch, Kendra occasionally comments on her own comments: "On still another hand, I realize that I should be an octopus if I have all these hands," she sighs after a particularly tortured argument with herself (*Harold*, 82). Kendra has what her Aunt Judy (who sounds a lot like Aunt Paula) calls a "smart-aleck mind" (*Harold*, 117). The novel is also full of life's little embarrassing moments, such as when Kendra gets soaked with water immediately upon being introduced to Frank. She also gets amusing letters throughout from her friends, who have been established as individuals early on.

Researching this book must have been a pleasure. Danziger played tourist and visited places on the scavenger hunt with her editor, including the Jewish Museum (twice) and many Mets games (but stopped when they kept losing). Not a soap opera fan, she toured the set of *All My Children* (she was friends with its lighting director) by herself; not satisfied with how her scene was going, she went back with a true fan and used her friend's perspective in making the scene come alive.

The book was done but untitled, and she was walking around singing all the New York songs she could think of, when the title hit her. One of her aims in this book was to publicize the good side of the city where she lived and to reduce its terrors: "I've never been mugged, and I've never mugged anyone," she likes to assure people. Ironically, however, she is now no longer as enamored of New York as she once was: "It doesn't seem to meet my needs anymore." London, home of the sequel to *Harold* (*Thames Doesn't Rhyme with James*), is her favorite city now, and she is picturing a dual life in Woodstock and London.

In reviewing *Harold*, *Publishers Weekly* especially liked its treatment of New York: "With characteristic humor, tart language, and quick phrasing, Danziger's teenagers not only share a summer getting to know each other but also explore the riches of a city often perceived as dirty and dangerous."[8] The *Voice of Youth Advocates* agreed, terming the scavenger hunt "a clever way of emphasizing civic awareness."[9] *Kirkus Reviews* felt the opposite, that the New York tour was vague and superficial; but they were becoming more of a fan of Danziger's "cheery, sympathetic" style, admiring the "rapid-fire puns delivered by a cast of sane characters willing to recognize problems and talk things out."[10] *School Library Journal* liked the "realistic characters, believable dialog, and smooth style."[11]

Harold is dedicated to Danziger's brother Barry (who served as the model for the younger brother in her first novel) and his family. And in a case of life coming full circle, Barry's son Sam was coming more and more to act as Danziger's "technical consultant"—especially with the irrepressibly high-spirited hero of her next four books.

7. The Matthew Martin Books

Matthew Martin: He is eleven years old (in just a minute). Is the youngest kid in his sixth grade class, and always striving to compensate. Lives in Califon, New Jersey. Is terrific with computers. Is horrific with spelling. Loves junk food. Loves tormenting his sister, age thirteen, whose troubles we sometimes see through his eyes. Hates being bored. Has a lawyer father and a health-food-nut mother who works for a place that delivers singing telegrams. Is rowdy, but tries to be endearing and sometimes succeeds. Is a firm believer in the "not fair" theory of life. Is always, always in trouble.

With her four books about Matthew Martin (named for comedian Dean), Danziger shifts into a whole new gear for her: telling stories from a boy's perspective. Possibly to make the shift more realistic (readers know she has never been a boy), she makes another major shift at the same time—into third person. All of her novels up until this have been of a piece: first person, present tense. Perhaps it is a sign of her decreasing anger over the years that she has come out of herself and can see other people in a third-person, more objective way.

In any case, the Matthew books are still in present tense, but they are aimed at a younger age group, the nine- to twelve-year-old set, with a male protagonist who is younger than any of Danziger's girls. This allows Danziger to take a new tack with her usual anguished thirteen-year-old girl, in this case Amanda Martin, who we now view through a pesky younger brother's eyes (much as Danziger's younger brother might have viewed her). Matthew can plainly see what lies ahead and can only hope he does not get as "weird" as Amanda when he becomes a teen. Amanda and Matthew snarl and backbite and insult each other to the nth degree, but they are deep-down fond of each other and can be affectionate; it is even foreshadowed that they will get along in the future (as the Danziger siblings do today). Amanda also occasionally allies with the adults in the narrative, to form a bemused, sort of Beverly Cleary overview of Matthew's exuberant naïveté: "Trouble," Matthew thinks as his teacher strides into the room mysteriously—"I have a feeling that there is something I have not done."[1]

Everyone Else's Parents Said Yes (1989)

Everyone Else's Parents Said Yes focuses shrewdly on the five days leading up to Matthew's eleventh-birthday bash, to which he is inviting all of his male pals. He is the type of boy who keeps a computer printout of his birthday countdown, announcing in the novel's first paragraph that "there are only five more days, fifteen hours, and thirty-two minutes until my birthday party" (*Parents*, 1).

He is also the type of boy who has alienated not one, not two, but every single girl in his sixth grade class. He puts bubble gum in Zoe's long blond hair. He makes fun of Jill, who has changed her name to Jil! to make herself more exciting. He refuses to admit that Chloe is as good on the computer as he is. He sends an SBD ("Silent But Deadly") expulsion of gas Vanessa's way, convincing the class that she is the "world's worst smeller" (*Parents*, 53). After Vanessa swears revenge, he devises a plan to collect "belly-button lint and toe crud from all of the boys" and put it in her desk (*Parents*, 81).

To punish him for such "sneaky, disgusting, and rotten" behavior (*Parents*, 61), the girls form an organization called GET HIM (for "Girls Eager To Halt Immature Matthew"). Worry about how they might ruin his party adds to his other party problems: How to get his mother, whose idea of fun is alfalfa sprouts and tofu, to agree to ice cream and cake, not to mention Gummy Worms, M&Ms, and licorice. How to make up with his best friend Joshua, who accidentally pulled the plug on Matthew's elaborate computerized invitations that he had slaved over (but had not stored). How to avoid the overwhelming temptation to sabotage his sister's first date, which is taking place on the night of his party.

The night finally arrives: "Let the wild rumpus begin!" shouts one boy, in homage to Maurice Sendak's *Where the Wild Things Are* (*Parents*, 95). All ends well, as Matthew receives great presents, has fun, and after finally breaking down and apologizing for his rudenesses, inadvertently becomes host of his sixth grade's first boy-girl party.

Most interesting of all, after all this time of scorning girls, he suddenly sees Jil! in a new light and realizes that she is a lot of fun when she is not picking on him. He starts counting down the days till his *next* birthday, and his parents exchange a look: "What will Matthew do next?" (*Parents*, 115). Sequels were already in the works to answer the question.

The title for this first Matthew book—the universal complaint from child to parent—came about as Danziger was writing dialogue for another character. It struck her as "too perfect," and she rewrote the line to fit Matthew, which it does—several times throughout the story.

The novel is blithe-spirited and not particularly "bibliotherapeutic." Perhaps it came as a relief to Danziger not to have to carry the burden of the older sibling this time: "I'm having the *best* time writing it," she said in an interview while she was working on this book. "When I'm the 'sister'—first person—I miss that younger brother character. I can understand both characters this way."[2]

It is easy to see where Matthew gets much of his sense of play. His father (especially for a lawyer—and a practicing one, unlike Danziger's own father) is more playful than most kids. One of the "good fathers" that Danziger thinks of as balancing her earlier ones, this one bonds with Matthew in their fondness for sugary foods; he cheers Matthew up with a boisterous romp of bubble-blowing; and he puts up with a lot more than most fathers would: "Disciplining his children is not one of Mr. Martin's favorite things about being a father" (*Parents*, 87). Matthew's mother has her moments also, as when donning some of her bizarre costumes from her singing telegram job. Frequent references to "that old TV Show" *Leave It to Beaver* are reminders that this is a real family and a "weird" one at that (as Amanda tries to explain to her date). And the stability of the Martin marriage provides security, unlike the home lives of Matthew's friends, many of whom are children of messy divorces.

Critical response to the Matthew books has been generally positive, with some quibbles. *American Bookseller* warmed to *Everyone Else's Parents* as "Danziger's first book about a boy" that would "have any brother nodding in agreement while chortling."[3] The *Bulletin of the Center for Children's Books* decided that no matter what the age group, Danziger was "incapable, apparently, of writing a book that isn't funny and lively," despite this one's "stretched" story line and the occasional "unpleasantness" of Matthew as a character.[4]

Booklist missed the "substantive issues found in her earlier works," but predicted that the book would have no trouble reaching its target audience: "Brisk in style and pacing, this lighthearted offering is sure to be popular."[5] *Kirkus* echoed: "Sure to entertain."[6] *School Library Journal* cheered that "in this book, readers meet a boy who they'll feel they already know" and that "sibling rivalry and parent/child conflicts are humorously yet realistically portrayed."[7] *Publishers Weekly* observed that Danziger "combines insight and humor in her first book for younger readers," with characters that "come alive through natural dialogue and universal experiences."[8]

To help with all the Matthew books, Danziger has gotten expert guidance from her nephew Sam Danziger, nine years old at the time of the first book, and his two brothers. While they are Califon, New Jersey, residents themselves, Danziger did not especially model Matthew on her nephews; Matthew, like all her characters, is a composite. Sam is acknowledged at the beginning of *Everyone Else's Parents*, along with "kids all over the country who have shared their ideas, experiences, and suggestions." With these books, each spaced only a year apart, Danziger seems to feel closer to her readers than ever.

Make Like a Tree and Leave (1990)

The second Matthew book was called *Matthew in the Middle*—"a terrible title," says Danziger—right up until the day she was delivering her manuscript to the publisher. She had arranged to meet a friend for lunch, and she found out that someone else was going to be there whom she did not like. She said to herself that if she was not having a good time, she could always "make like a tree and leave"—and suddenly she had her title. (The phrase was also used as a throwaway line in *Remember Me to Harold Square* [*Harold*, 89]).

In *Make Like a Tree and Leave* the title line comes out of the mouth of Amanda, whose sparring with Matthew grows ever fiercer. He does awful things, like writing comments in her private diary, and she retaliates. He is the one who sees a way to a temporary truce, however, when he notices that she calls him "honey baby" when she needs a favor and yells things like "make like a tree and leave" on all the other days. "This tree is not planning on leaving anytime soon. . . . I have just as much right to be here as you do," he tells her seriously.[9] Then he does the favor she has requested, and "Amanda admits to herself that there are moments when she actually likes her younger brother" (*Tree*, 107).

The novel opens with perhaps the ultimate in Matthew's comic disasters. As chairman of the Mummy Committee for Egyptian Feast Day at school, he leads the way in helping his two friends wrap the fourth comrade, the luckless Brian, in wet gauze. Matthew is trying to be responsible, even worrying about whether he will be able to perform the Heimlich maneuver if his friend keeps eating while he is being encased. It is a situation that allows for plenty of gross jokes, and then catastrophe, when Brian appears permanently trapped in his full-length plaster body cast. Will he get out before his bladder explodes? How much trouble has Matthew brought down on his head this time?

Even with help from others, including his mother in a gorilla costume and his sister with half-crinkled hair, Matthew ends up in a doctor's office, where Brian is surgically excised. Lectures to Matthew take place offstage, which allows the action to keep rolling.

Subplots abound as Mrs. Nichols, everyone's favorite seventy-eight-year-old, breaks her hip and is in danger of losing her land. Matthew and others concoct plans, including a hair-raising pet wash, to raise money for a conservancy that will take over the property and preserve it. Most puzzling (to Matthew) of all is the way Jil! is starting to look so cute, and how he could have gone from thinking girls were "slug slime" one month to wanting to call one the next. The novel ends with their exchanging their first spontaneous hug.

Matthew's father continues to be a pal. He tries not force but reason to stop the sibling rivalry by quoting Martin Luther King Jr. ("We must live together as brothers or perish as fools" [*Tree*, 57]), and he answers the phone with "This is the Martin Home for the Chronically Bonzo. Head warden speaking" (*Tree*, 71). At one point, he pulls Matthew away from his dreaded closet cleaning to take a popcorn break. Soon the entire kitchen is popping; Matthew has given his father the wrong measurements.

Even funnier is that Danziger, when having Mrs. Martin give the "correct" recipe a few pages later, also gets it wrong ("one tablespoon of oil takes one-third of a cup" [*Tree*, 40]) and has gotten polite letters pointing out the error. "Don't ask me math questions," she warns. (Another glitch in the Matthew books is the occasional inconsistency, a pitfall in series books. The Martin parents meet in college in one book, while in another the meeting takes place in third grade.)

More research went into the story Mrs. Martin tells about her first pair of contact lenses: "I was making out with my boyfriend and he swallowed one of the lenses" (*Tree*, 41). This was the answer Danziger got when she called her eye doctor to ask for his funniest contact lens story. (He is thanked in the acknowledgments.)

Despite some carping, reviewers unanimously praised the comedy in *Make Like a Tree and Leave*: "As she is prone to do, Danziger offers too many situations and characters for good continuity," wrote *Booklist*. "However, her fans probably won't notice or won't mind—they'll be laughing too hard."[10]

"Readers are sure to appreciate the humor," added *School Library Journal*,[11] while *Kirkus* commented that Danziger "continues to have a precise ear for the pungencies of grade-school humor."[12] *Publishers Weekly* accurately points out that "Danziger's novels are like cotton candy: they're fun and light, and children positively gobble them up."[13]

With these books, Danziger has traveled considerable distance from the anger in *The Cat Ate My Gymsuit*. Perhaps it is a distance created by being closer now to her niece's and nephews' growing up, rather than to her own teen years. The "I hate my father" cry for help in *Cat* has over the years turned into an excuse for a joke, as when the Martin parents try to figure out when Amanda stopped being their sweet little girl: "I think it was about the time the 'I hate my parents' hormone developed. In the psychology books it's called adolescence onset" (*Tree*, 72). Now the thirteen-year-old character's angst is not under a microscope, but seen from a distance—mainly as an example that is *not* giving Matthew confidence in his own looming adolescence.

Earth to Matthew (1991)

In *Make Like a Tree* Amanda undergoes fashion permutations (dressing in all black) that by *Earth to Matthew*, the third book of the Matthew Martin series, turn a little grim. She takes to wearing motifs of skulls and bones, lots of safety pins, two-tone hair, and then a nose ring. Finally, she shaves off all her hair—Amanda has gone punk.

Perhaps she is a 1990s version of Marcy Lewis after all, as Mrs. Martin points out: "You're angry all the time. Nothing we do pleases you."[14] Is she on drugs? No, she is just unhappy because no one understands her. Eventually she is in the same place as

Marcy: in therapy, along with her parents and most reluctant brother.

The therapy scenes are not shown; we are only meant to appreciate the wisdom of Mr. and Mrs. Martin in realizing they need outside help with Amanda. What is in the foreground in *Earth to Matthew* is our hero as he bumbles his way through the ups and downs of sixth grade romance. "Earth to Matthew" is Jil!'s subtle method of getting Matthew "Trouble Is My Middle Name" Martin to focus on her. It is a tough job; he is busy smashing cupcakes into Vanessa's chest (causing her T-shirt to go from "Born to Shop" to "Born to hop") and ducking Jil!'s dad, who videotapes *everything*.

This book gives Danziger the delicious opportunity to present a first date from the boy's point of view, with all its worries, like: "What should he do in between those two events, the beginning and the end?" (*Earth*, 55). She also has a character try out a technique learned from *Oprah*—when Jil! finally tells her father to give her some privacy.

In school the kids are learning all about ecosystems (which Matthew thinks of as "echo-systems"), allowing Danziger to weave in lot of teen-appropriate environmental facts as well as plenty of jokes about diapers and toilets. A trip at the end of sixth grade rewards the budding ecologists with an overnight stay at the Franklin Institute in Philadelphia, an event full of assorted comic traumas.

Families are ecosystems, too, as Matthew finds out, though it is hard for the reader to see just where the Martin parents could have gone wrong with Amanda. Mr. Martin is more of a pal than ever; not only is he always asking how Matthew feels, but they plan activities together every Saturday and straightforwardly call it "Boy-Bonding Time" (*Earth*, 2).

Besides the hint of significant family trouble, there is another serious moment when Matthew and Jil! talk about the "depressing" vastness of the earth's environmental problems. But after pledging to do what they can to help save the planet, they cheer up and Matthew is soon making "devil's horns" behind Jil!'s head—in sixth grade, a sign of true love.

Earth to Matthew has an all-boy feel to it—like the "Beavis and Butt-head" cartoon show on MTV or Wayne and Garth's wit from *Wayne's World*—juvenile but undeniably funny. There is doubtless good reason it is dedicated to Samuel Anthony Danziger, "Terrific Nephew and a great Consultant."

Reviewers were appreciative. "A total triumph and complete delight," wrote *School Library Journal*.[15] The *Bulletin of the Center for Children's Books* argued: "Bright, breezy style and a good ear for dialogue compensate for the fact that the incidents and relationships are not tied by a strong story line."[16] *Kirkus* concluded: "This third Matthew story stands alone, but will have readers asking for the others."[17]

Not for a Billion Gazillion Dollars (1992)

Danziger's readers get a fourth Matthew story in *Not for a Billion Gazillion Dollars*. As summer vacation begins, Matthew knows what he needs more than anything in the world: the latest computer graphics program that, unfortunately, costs big bucks, or at least bigger ones than he has. As his frantic search for money unfurls, we learn that Matthew already owes it—to his parents, to Jil!, and to an entire three-quarters of his class.

Problems with Amanda, his "sister from Hell," have faded into the background (as perhaps all younger brothers wish older sisters would). She is away at Camp Sarah Bernhardt, trying to put her flair for the dramatic to use as a future career.

Family counseling has worked swiftly, and Mr. and Mrs. Martin have decided to become stricter parents. Yet this may be the book where Danziger finally gives parents a break. Maybe Amanda's woes are not parentally induced after all: "I don't know why everything seems so hard all of a sudden. No. You're not *that* terrible as parents," she says in answer to their anxious question.[18]

That is a speech Danziger may not have been able to write some twenty years ago. Thirteen-year-olds just plain have problems, she seems to say here, problems inexplicable and on a much vaster scale than whatever their merely mortal "parental units" have done.

Developments with Jil! continue to mount, most deliciously when Matthew looks at her head as she bends over the drinking fountain, thinking fondly how a few months earlier he would have pushed it into the fountain; then he takes a drink and Jil! pushes *his* head into the fountain. These and many other incidents are meant to sympathize with nine- to twelve-year-olds as they navigate the perils of the contemporary romance-maze while approaching their teen years, as they are reading older brothers' *Playboys*, realizing it is sometimes more fun to think about kissing than to actually do it, and getting conflicting advice from every corner.

Danziger has a lot of fun with Matthew's moneymaking schemes, from begging (too unproductive) and lawn mowing (too boring) to baby-sitting (too drenched with bodily substances) and washing car windshields (too dangerous), and finally to designing computerized business and greeting cards (just right). Something mysterious is happening to Matthew as he moves along. Without ever coming out and saying so, Danziger adroitly has him maturing and learning to think of others besides himself. He learns a hard lesson about money, too, that it has to be earned and there is no magic way to get it.

In a nice touch, his parents reveal *their* former compulsive spending and credit-card bingeing, and Matthew realizes that the whole subject is a lot more complex than a kid thinks at first: "Matthew knows that he doesn't want to deal with all of this money stuff—not even for a billion gazillion dollars. He also knows that he has no choice" (*Billion*, 73). Wisdom about money (especially the fact that it is not equivalent to having credit cards) is something even many adults fail to attain, and Danziger handles the subject realistically, humorously, and sanely here. In a final, truly nice stroke, she has Matthew donate his extra earnings to UNICEF, in part because Jil! has awakened him to the sorrows of needy children, and in part because he is seeing on his own that generosity is part of growing up.

Autobiographical touches in this book include "gazillion" (one of Danziger's favorite words—perhaps appropriately, for a math-impaired writer or for one with a flair for exaggeration), and a certain fascination with snot bubble gum (a suitcase full of it once got her stopped going through customs).

Publishers Weekly was pleased to note that in this fourth Matthew book, "Danziger has sustained the boy's high energy level and sharp sense of humor." It praised the "vibrant, present-tense narrative, characteristically overflowing with puns, jibes and jokes, once again [demonstrating] that this talented author knows what makes kids tick—and what makes them laugh."[19]

Over the course of four books—which do stand alone but are even better when taken together, to be read as a four-part continuous saga with developing themes and characters—Matthew has become a much more sympathetic protagonist. He once was a rowdy tormenter of girls, pretty much a pain in the neck with lots of energy and creativity. Now his gifts are going into positive directions. His parents may poke fun ("I feel a *Leave It to Beaver* moment coming on," jokes his dad [*Billion*, 116]), but they acknowledge aloud what we have already seen: Matthew has become someone to be proud of, lovable and thoughtful. It is a mark of Danziger's skill that she is able to sustain this gradual growth wholly believably over not one book, but four.

"I really love Matthew," she wrote at the same time she was working on the last book. "One of the things I like best is that he grows and changes in the books, develops a social conscience while still maintaining a high sense of play. A high sense of play is something that I value in myself, so I really like it in Matthew."[20]

With the conclusion of his final book, Matthew has survived a year in Danziger's capable hands and resourcefully faces adulthood—or at least the seventh grade.

8. Amber Brown and the Future

Surviving through humor is Paula Danziger's trademark theme. But surviving what? There is never a shortage of things for a young adult to survive, but what Danziger most concerns herself with is injustice, in all its permutations, in the adult world. In this respect she aligns her attitudes with the perennial themes of children's literature. The novelist Avi, author of two Newbery Honor books (*The True Confessions of Charlotte Doyle* and *Nothing But the Truth*, about another classroom patriotism controversy), has written:

> Fiction in children's literature is about unfairness, inconsistency, and lack of justice in the adult world. The constant struggle to adjust good with bad. Save us, we are saying to the children, save us from what you are becoming. Save us from what we are teaching you to become. The ultimate irony is that the plots of children's literature fiction are more often than not about the passage into adulthood. So, children's literature is a cry for help from adults to children.[1]

"Unfairness" and the "lack of justice in the adult world" are the constant undercurrents of Danziger's work. Her protagonists start out powerless, in a situation they can see only as disadvantageous to them. They are frequently angry and bitter about it until they start recognizing the power within themselves. Danziger adds humor to the brew, in part because her funny bone never sleeps, but also to prevent her books from becoming pure bibliotherapy and—speaking frankly—to get her books *read*.

With her use of irony and wit, and expressing self-deprecation rather than lashing out, Danziger's stories spring from a long tradition that includes J. D. Salinger's *The Catcher in the Rye*, Louise Fitzhugh's *Harriet the Spy*, Beverly Cleary's Ramona books, and many others, going all the way back to Mark Twain's *Huckleberry Finn*. Her characters defy authority, try to assert control over their own lives, and make that passage from believing they are the center of the universe to finding a place in the social structure, all the while retaining their integrity. This is what we call growing up.

Just as perceived injustice and unfairness have been the frequent themes in her novels, they have also been the themes in her life, or at least her life as a child now recollected and interpreted in adulthood. To paraphrase Wordsworth: "The daughter is mother of the woman." To quote Danziger: "Everything in my life offers a connection to my writing and some [things] have more of an impact than others."[2]

Thus Danziger, with care and integrity, uses her creativity to hone each element of her novels so that they hit home with their intended audience. At the same time, perhaps, she is inventing characters to wage war on issues with which one never really stops wrestling. She is using her smart and sensitive characters, more often than not female, to fight her battles for her, to cry out to both children and the child within herself: "Watch out, or you'll end up like *them*—the hypocritical adult establishment! Take care, or you'll become part of the problem, not the solution!" It is a cry for help that fits squarely within the tradition of the best of children's literature, the books that last.

Amber Brown Is Not a Crayon (1994)

With her newest books, about feisty Amber Brown of New Jersey, Danziger is reaching an even younger age group with her themes and humor. Amber is in the third grade, and the books about her are chapter books—a comparatively new genre considered to be a bridge between picture books and middle-grade novels, for ages six to nine. Chapter books are the first books children read that are divided into separate chapters, with larger-than-usual print and one or several illustrations per chapter. The challenge to the writer is to extend the attention span of second-through-fourth graders by using deceptively simple language to capture their interest. Not a word can be wasted, snappy dialogue is essential, and humor is always a plus—three particular strengths of Danziger's writing.

Amber Brown Is Not a Crayon, published in 1993 in England and in 1994 in the United States, is not, however, an all-out funny story: it concerns a girl who is forced to deal with her best friend leaving. The story started out as a picture book written for Danziger's niece Carrie, then ten, at a time when *her* best friend moved away. To cheer her up, Danziger wrote a two-page piece about coping with loss. Afterward, she realized that the pages were more about herself; they were also about what she wanted to say to a good friend then dying from AIDS. With a mind of its own, the piece evolved into its present form as a book of nine chapters, dedicated to "Carrie Marie Danziger, niece, consultant, and pal."

Narrated in Danziger's usual mode—first person, present tense—the story begins with all the ways having Justin Daniels for a best friend makes life better. He sits with Amber in school, usually knows what she is thinking, entertains and defends her, helps her with math—and she does equally important things for him. They are a great team (or even marriage), though Justin is in transit, waiting for his parents' house to sell so the family will be reunited in far-off Alabama, where his father has a new job. In part an account of a celebrated friendship, this book never veers into sentimentality or makes a big deal of the sad rarity of boy-girl friendships in the third grade (or of their uncommonly creative, sympathetic teacher—a man).

Also downplayed is that Amber is another "child of divorce," living with her mother while her father is off working in France, halfway across the world. It is never stressed, for example, that one reason Amber feels the loss of Justin so keenly is that it is following right on the heels of the loss of her father. Knowing that now her best friend is moving away makes her almost physically ill. The way Danziger conveys this, in the unpretentious language of sadness, will pull palpably at the heartstrings of almost any reader who has ever suffered a loss. Amber has a new twist on the universal complaint: "Life sure isn't fair some days—some years."[3]

Amber is willing to deal head-on with the imminent separation, but the tension increases when Justin is not. The friends stop speaking even before Justin leaves town. Twice in this short book Danziger uses well the technique she first learned from Shirley Jackson, that of bringing back something mentioned earlier and having it gather new meaning. In the beginning there is a scene where Amber talks about her and Justin's love of pizza, their "favorite food group" (*Crayon*, 29). Whenever they hear one being ordered, they always yell, "And hold the anchovies"— cracking up while picturing a poor guy who actually has to hold them. This bit of clowning becomes important at the end, when a pizza gets ordered and Amber finally breaks the ice by calling "Hold the anchovies" (*Crayon*, 69)—their way of getting back together after their big fight and enjoying what little time they have left.

There is also the ball of used chewing gum they have been carefully accumulating for a year and a half. It is a declaration of war when Justin, following his mom's orders to prune his possessions, throws out the ball of gum even when he knows it will upset Amber. Then, when he is finally ready to say he is going to miss her, he retrieves and makes her a present of the ball, and in Danziger's amazing way, she turns this into a genuinely touching moment between kids. It could even make a reader cry—if that gum were not such a disgusting image.

It is a bittersweet ending. They face their loss directly, and Amber realizes that her powerlessness may be fierce, like that of all Danziger heroines, but it is only temporary. She takes comfort in thinking "about how it will be when Justin and I grow up and he doesn't have to move just because his parents move" (*Crayon*, 74). Meanwhile, he is her third grade hero, and he will always live on in her memory that way.

Amber has an Aunt Pamela who sounds eerily similar to an Aunt Paula, and a mom who uses food in a way that psychologists would not approve—offering uncooked brownie mix as solace during times of trouble. But unlike many of Danziger's previous parental figures, this mother also is a good listener, and Amber is appreciative: "I'm so lucky to have a mother who doesn't act like my feelings don't count, just because I'm a kid" (*Crayon*, 64).

The title of the book comes from the teasing about her name she sometimes gets (and hates): "Amber Brown is not a crayon. Amber Brown is a person," she insists (*Crayon*, 20). She loves her name and will defend it to the death from cracks about crayon colors from "goofballs" and "tuna-heads." Treasuring her identity, she has taken great strides beyond older Danziger heroines.

The first Amber book has generated some of the most positive critical commentary of Danziger's entire career: "There's lots of fun along with the pathos here," noted *School Library Journal* in a starred review. "Danziger reaches out to a younger audience in this funny, touching slice of third-grade life, told in the voice of a feisty, lovable heroine."[4] *Booklist* commended the author for getting Amber's "funny and vulnerable voice" down pat "without a trace of condescension" and called her friendship with Justin "beautifully drawn."[5] Even *Kirkus* was unexpectedly effusive: "It's grand to have Danziger add books for younger readers to her many popular titles for the older crowd."[6] And *Publishers Weekly*, in another starred review, credited Danziger with adding "to her oeuvre's sizable brood of magnetic young characters": "Once again, Danziger demonstrates her ability to connect with her audience. One hopes she has more escapades planned for Amber."[7]

You Can't Eat Your Chicken Pox, Amber Brown (1995)

Indeed, a second Amber title was already in the works. Called *You Can't Eat Your Chicken Pox, Amber Brown*, the sequel was again inspired by Danziger's niece. Carrie, while in Danziger's care in London, had what she thought were bug bites—which turned out to be chicken pox. Amber, while getting ready for her summer vacation in London, is proud that though everyone else in class has been plagued with chicken pox, she herself never catches anything except fireflies. She starts scratching at "bug bites" even before she gets out of the country, but it is not until London that the "pox plague" fully invades, leaving Aunt Pam to cope.

The second Amber book brings to the fore another potentially sad topic—being a child of divorced parents. With her parents separated only six months, Amber experiences common reactions that the characters in *The Divorce Express* and *It's an Aardvark-Eat-Turtle World* have lived with a long time or already outgrown. She keeps a secret "Dad Book" of photos of the family back when she *thought* everyone was happy. She occasionally forgets that her parents have split up. She still thinks they will get back together—the favorite fantasy of children of divorce.

Even when she falls ill and feels she might die, she speculates about how her misfortune could be used to get her parents back together. But reality always hits: Her dad in France is reachable only by phone, and her mother is dating a new man who knows more about Amber than she knows about him.

Amber has been hurt; her life is never going to be the same, and her parents' poor communication leads to a crisis when her father finally does make an appearance in her life, arriving in London post–chicken pox. No wonder Amber just wants to be a kid again. Crisis resolved, her father says he will get transferred back to New York and promises better communication in the future.

Throughout, Amber's "perky" patter never ceases, keeping the book light. She is surviving with a sense of humor, even at age eight. She is actually somewhat more in control of her life than the characters in Danziger's earlier divorce books. She ends up still loving both parents—but actively, advising them to take "marriage lessons" (and even "divorce lessons") if they plan to marry anyone else.

Before and after the pox, Amber gets in a little London sightseeing. This being a Danziger tour, events include having a pigeon at Trafalgar Square land on Amber's head and rip out some of her hair as it escapes; getting stuck in the elevator at the flat; being hit in the head by camera bags at Buckingham Palace; and dropping her iced tea at the Hard Rock Cafe, turning her T-shirt into a "tea-shirt." Readers pick up facts about London even when Amber is bedridden, from the marathons of Monopoly, British version, that she plays.

There is a purely autobiographical touch when Amber decides to practice her signature for her eventual certain fame, at just about the same age as her creator began doing the same thing. Aunt Pam herself is a breezy, flamboyant character who calls her niece "Amberino"—a terrific companion, though a little out of her depth when she is called upon for more intensive child care than she planned.

The title comes from a letter Amber receives from good old Justin in Alabama, who reminds her about that kid in kindergarten who tried to eat his chicken pox scabs because he thought they looked like candy. In advising her not to do the same (he is still looking out for her), he makes Amber remember all over again how much she misses him. Danziger comments that "no grown-up likes the title of this book—too gross. But it's perfect." In case the grown-ups overruled her, she came up with a safer alternative (*Everything's a Joke with You, Amber Brown*), but luckily she did not have to use it.

Danziger loves the name Amber Brown (and has a great deal of fun repeating it in the books), though it represents a departure: All of the major characters in her books are named after comedians except Amber, and she says that it is "scary" to break that tradition. At present, Danziger plans at least three more Amber books, taking her into fourth grade, with working titles of *Amber Brown Goes Fourth*, *Amber Brown Sees Red*, and *4ever Amber Brown*.

Kids who discover and get to know Amber Brown will most likely be on the lookout for Danziger's titles for young adults as they get older and graduate from chapter books. When they find themselves gobbling up *The Cat Ate My Gymsuit*, *The Divorce Express*, or *Not for a Billion Gazillion Dollars*, they are going to enjoy being in familiar territory—or interested to find that they are in for a surprise or two after all.

Thames Doesn't Rhyme with James (1994)

Hot off the press is a second love song to London, Danziger's new home for part of each year, in the form of a return to young adult novel territory. The long-awaited sequel to *Remember Me to Harold Square*, entitled *Thames Doesn't Rhyme with James*, took seven years in real time, but picks up just a few months after the first book leaves off. Chock-full of fun facts, the new story takes Kendra, Frank, and company on their promised reward-trip to London at Christmastime. In between taking part in yet another scavenger hunt and mastering British pronunciation, Kendra spends much time wanting her parents to treat her more like a grown-up, trying to figure out who she is and what she wants, and perfecting kissing techniques with Frank. At the story's end, though Kendra is about to return to New York City while Frank heads back to Wisconsin, she is several steps closer to independence on a perfect New Year's Eve.

Publishers Weekly praised the novels "consistently droll repartee" and judged the second book a fitting companion for its predecessor: "Danziger's witty sequel to *Remember Me to Harold Square* has all of the zip of that novel—plus the historically rich setting of London."[8] A third book about Kendra is in the planning stages, another love song to London tentatively titled *Seen It, Done It, Got the T-shirt*.

Illustrating her continued close connection to family—and also the longevity of her career—Danziger dedicates *Thames Doesn't Rhyme with James* to her youngest nephew, Josh, "who wasn't born when *Remember Me to Harold Square* was dedicated to the rest of the family."

Speaking about her life now, "having written the fifteen books for children and young adults I have been exploring and having dealt head-on with the major problems of her life," Danziger has a predominant feeling of gratitude, as opposed to her previous anger: "How grateful I am for so much in my life and how terrific it is to be doing something that I care about," she says. "I feel that this living—I know this is going to sound trite and New Age but so what—is all part of a journey. There are all the things I look forward to doing, and I want to do lots of different writing."

Danziger has known for as long as she has been a writer that she is someday going to write a book called *Pardon My Two Left Wheels* about a kid in a wheelchair. Because she herself has dealt with casts, crutches, and braces, she likes speaking to classes of physically challenged kids—"the label doesn't matter, they're people."

She probably will *not* be writing any animal stories—"they don't do funny enough things." There are several artists she is interested in collaborating with, and she plans to continue her TV show and speaking engagements. As far as those activities that take time away from her writing—"I don't care. We're all creative people, whatever we do expresses that. These things make my experience much deeper."

The educational "establishment" is not always on Danziger's side, but that is not a problem over which she appears to lose sleep. An interviewer once chided her for an apparent lack of classical education, to which Danziger shot back, "I like rock-and-roll."[9] Maintaining her integrity is important, but critical applause is not necessarily Danziger's biggest goal, and indeed she has written a whole article called "Why I Will Never Win the Newbery Medal."[10] Instead, she says, "what I strive for is that rush of recognition you get from friends—the kind of connection you get when you say something funny and you know that *they* get it."[11]

In some ways, Danziger's books appear to bypass the adult critical establishment altogether, reaching readers directly through enormous paperback sales. "Few critics would place Paula Danziger's novels in the pantheon of YA fiction," write fellow critics Alleen Pace Nilsen and Kenneth L. Donelson, "yet Danziger is among the most popular writers for young adults." Why? Because her books "do not talk down to their readers," they present "real issues and real problems," and they "do not pretend there are easy answers." Most important, perhaps, "her humor is exactly what her readers want"—no matter what objections adult critics hurl at her.[12]

One of the most frequent objections—that the books are clichéd and do not stretch readers' imaginations—is in this sense beside the point. Readers gobble up these kind of books—when they are well done—to be reassured, to confirm who they are during adolescence, that difficult time when more than ever you do not know who you are.

In Danziger's case, millions of books sold mean that millions of readers *are* getting the kind of connection she strives for—and that success is hers. Or, to put it another way, in the recent words of a CNN reporter, "Paula Danziger is *definitely* an author you'd want around your house."[13]

Notes and References

Preface

1.   Kathleen Krull, "A Once-Upon-a-Time Quiz," *New York Times Book Review*, 8 November 1987, 32.

1. Survival Through Humor (1944–1969)

1.   Unless otherwise noted, quotations from Paula Danziger throughout the book are from interviews conducted by the author in 1992–1994; a transcript of an interview conducted by Ann Durell in 1987 (used with permission of Paula Danziger); and speeches either seen by the author or supplied on videotape by Paula Danziger.

2.   Jean Richardson, "The Danziger Blitz," *Publishers Weekly*, 19 July 1991, 37.

3.   Paula Danziger, *The Pistachio Prescription* (New York: Dell Publishing, 1978), 57; hereafter cited in the text as *Pistachio*.

4.   Mark Twain, *Fenimore Cooper's Literary Offenses* (1895).

5.   Lenny Bruce, *The Essential Lenny Bruce* (New York: Ballantine Publishers, 1967), epigraph.

6.   Robert O. Boorstin, *New York Times*, 2 April 1986.

2. Let the Writing Begin (1970–1994)

1.   *Something About the Author Autobiography Series*, vol. 36 (Detroit: Gale Research Company, 1984), 63.

2.   Paula Danziger, "I Followed the Sweet Potato," *Voice of Youth Advocates*, June 1979, 8.

3. The Marcy Lewis Books

1.   J. D. Reed, "Packaging the Facts of Life," *Time*, 23 August 1982, 65.

2. Paula Danziger, *The Cat Ate My Gymsuit* (New York: Dell Publishing, 1974), 2; hereafter cited in the text as *Cat*.

3. Reed, "Packaging the Facts of Life," 65.

4. Dennis Freeland, "A Conversation with Paula Danziger," *Writing!*, November 1988, 20.

5. Perry Nodelman, "How Typical Children Read Typical Books," *Children's Literature in Education*, Winter 1981, 177–85.

6. *Kirkus Reviews*, 15 November 1974, 1206.

7. Veronica Geng, *New York Times Book Review*, 5 January 1975, 8.

8. *School Library Journal*, 15 November 1975, 1206.

9. *Booklist*, 1 November 1990.

10. Paula Danziger, *There's a Bat in Bunk Five* (New York: Dell Publishing, 1980), 1; hereafter cited in the text as *Bat*.

11. Paula Danziger, "If My Life Were a Novel," Dell Publishing brochure, 1980.

12. Natalie Babbitt, *New York Times Book Review*, 23 November 1980, 36–37.

13. *School Library Journal*, January 1981, 68.

14. *Bulletin of the Center for Children's Books*, December 1980, 68.

15. *Something About the Author*, 63.

16. *Kirkus Reviews*, 1 January 1981, 12.

17. Paula Danziger, "The Danziger Prescription," *ALAN Review*, Fall 1979, 7.

4. A Way with Titles

1. Selma G. Lanes, *New York Times Book Review*, 18 March 1979, 26.

2. The sentiment of growth-toward-self-reliance expressed by this Camus quotation is a popular one with young adults—and with young adult authors. Robert Cormier used this quote as the source for the title of the unpublished novel that was the antecedent for *The Bumblebee Flies Anyway* (New York: Pantheon Books, 1983)—called *In the Midst of Winter*. Jean Ferris also found the quote inspirational in her young adult novel *Invincible Summer* (New York: Farrar Straus, 1987).

3. *Something About the Author*, 63.

4. Lanes, *New York Times Book Review*, 26.

5. *Booklist*, 15 April 1978, 1347.

6. *Kirkus Reviews*, 1 April 1978, 379.

7. Carol Haffke, "A Writer's Childhood Helps Tell the Tale," *Gold Coast Bulletin*, 16 June 1988.

8. Paula Danziger, *Can You Sue Your Parents for Malpractice?* (New York: Dell Publishing, 1979), 18; hereafter cited in the text as *Malpractice*.

9. Dennis Freeland, "Paula Danziger's Young Adult World," *Writer's Digest*, January 1990, 40.

10. Ibid.

11. *School Library Journal*, April 1979.

12. *Booklist*, 1 May 1979, 1361.

13. *Journal of Reading*, February 1980, 473.

14. Jane Langton, *New York Times Book Review*, 17 June 1979, 25.

5. Children of Divorce

1. Sandra Martin, "Kids Love Danziger and Her Funny, Feeling Books," *Toronto Globe and Mail*, 2 February 1982.

2. *Something About the Author*, 64.

3. Ibid.

4. Paula Danziger, *The Divorce Express* (New York: Dell Publishing, 1982), 1; hereafter cited in the text as *Divorce*.

5. *Horn Book*, October 1982, 516.

6. *Growing Point*, September 1986, 4674.

7. *Booklist*, 15 September 1982, 112.

8. *Bulletin of the Center for Children's Books*, September 1982, 6.

9. Diane Gersoni Edelman, *New York Times Book Review*, 13 February 1983, 30.

10. *Something About the Author*, 64.

11. Anne Tyler, *Washington Post*, 12 May 1985.

12. *Something About the Author*, 64.

13. Freeland, "Paula Danziger's Young Adult World," 78.

14. Paula Danziger, *It's an Aardvark-Eat-Turtle World* (New York: Dell Publishing, 1985), 4; hereafter cited in the text as *Aardvark*.

15. *Bulletin of the Center for Children's Books*, June 1985, 183.

16. *Voice of Youth Advocates*, June 1985, 129.

17. *School Library Journal*, April 1985, 96.

18. *Interracial Books for Children Bulletin*, Vol. 16, No. 8, 1985, 18.

6. From New York to Outer Space and Back Again

1. Paula Danziger, *This Place Has No Atmosphere* (New York: Dell Publishing, 1986), 29; hereafter cited in the text as *Atmosphere*.

2. *School Library Journal*, November 1986, 100.

3. *Horn Book*, March/April 1987, 208.

4. *Bulletin of the Center for Children's Books*, January 1987, 85.

5. *Kirkus Reviews*, 1 September 1986, 1368.

6. Paula Danziger, *Remember Me to Harold Square* (New York: Dell Publishing, 1987), 8; hereafter cited in the text as *Harold*.

7. *Bulletin of the Center for Children's Books*, November 1987, 46.

8.   *Publishers Weekly*, 8 August 1987, 105.
9.   *Voice of Youth Advocates*, December 1987, 233.
10. *Kirkus Reviews*, 1 September 1987, 1318.
11. *School Library Journal*, November 1987, 114.

7. The Matthew Martin Books

1.   Paula Danziger, *Everyone Else's Parents Said Yes* (New York: Dell Publishing, 1989), 51; hereafter cited in the text as *Parents*.
2.   Freeland, "Paula Danziger's Young Adult World," 78.
3.   *American Bookseller*, February 1990.
4.   *Bulletin of the Center for Children's Books*, February 1990, 134.
5.   *Booklist*, 1 October 1989, 347.
6.   *Kirkus Reviews*, 1 October 1989.
7.   *School Library Journal*, September 1989, 249.
8.   *Publishers Weekly*, 8 September 1989.
9.   Paula Danziger, *Make Like a Tree and Leave* (New York: Dell Publishing, 1990), 105; hereafter cited in the text as *Tree*.
10. *Booklist*, 1 August 1990.
11. *School Library Journal*, October 1990, 114.
12. *Kirkus Reviews*, 15 July 1990.
13. *Publishers Weekly*, 29 June 1990, 102.
14. Paula Danziger, *Earth to Matthew* (New York: Dell Publishing, 1991), 92; hereafter cited in the text as *Earth*.
15. *School Library Journal*, October 1991, 122.
16. *Bulletin of the Center for Children's Books*, September 1991.
17. *Kirkus Reviews*, 15 September 1991.
18. Paula Danziger, *Not for a Billion Gazillion Dollars* (New York: Dell Publishing, 1992), 19; hereafter cited in the text as *Billion*.
19. *Publishers Weekly*, 27 July 1992, 63.
20. Paula Danziger, "Presenting Paula Danziger," Dell Publishing brochure, 1991.

8. Amber Brown and the Future

1.   Avi, "The Child in Children's Literature," *Horn Book*, January/February 1993, 48.
2.   Paula Danziger and others, "Facets: Successful Authors Talk About Connections Between Teaching and Writing," *English Journal*, November 1984, 24–27.
3.   Paula Danziger, *Amber Brown Is Not a Crayon* (New York: Putnam, 1994), 38; hereafter cited in the text as *Crayon*.
4.   *School Library Journal*, May 1994.
5.   *Booklist*, 1 January 1994.

6. *Kirkus Reviews*, 1 March 1994.

7. *Publishers Weekly*, 21 February 1994, 254.

8. *Publishers Weekly*, 12 September 1994, 92.

9. Richardson, "The Danziger Blitz" (see chap. 1, n. 2).

10. Anonymous [Paula Danziger], "Why I Will Never Win the Newbery Medal," *Top of the News*, Fall 1979, 57–60.

11. Freeland, "A Conversation with Paula Danziger," 19.

12. Kenneth L. Donelson and Alleen Pace Nilsen, "Poetry, Drama, and Humor: Of Lines and Laughs," in their *Literature for Today's Young Adults* (Glenview, Ill.: Scott Foresman, 1985), 335–69.

13. Michele Ross, "Cover to Cover," broadcast on CNN, March 1994. The segment included praise of *Amber Brown Is Not a Crayon* as a "very funny book," and the comment that all of Danziger's works "are marked by a keen ear, an intuitive grasp of what's on the mind of children at various ages, and a steady dose of humor to move the stories along."

Appendix I:
Awards and Honors Won
by Paula Danziger

Can You Sue Your Parents for Malpractice?

New Jersey Institute of Technology Authors Award
Land of Enchantment Book Award (New Mexico)
"Children's Choices" list of the International Reading Association—
    Children's Book Council

The Cat Ate My Gymsuit

Nene Award, chosen by children of Hawaii
New Jersey Institute of Technology Authors Award
"Children's Choices" list of the International Reading Association—
    Children's Book Council
One of five finalists for the California Young Reader Medal
Massachusetts Children's Book Award

The Divorce Express

Parents' Choice magazine award

Everyone Else's Parents Said Yes

Parents' Choice magazine award

The Pistachio Prescription

Child Study Association Book of the Year
One of five finalists for the California Young Reader Medal
Nominated for Arizona Young Reader Award

"Children's Choices" list of the International Reading Association—
   Children's Book Council

There's a Bat in Bunk Five

California Young Reader Medal
"Children's Choices" list of the International Reading Association—
   Children's Book Council

Other Awards

The Multiple Sclerosis Read-a-thon Author of the Year for 1982 and
   1983
One of five finalists for British Book Award for Children's Book Author
   of the Year, 1993

Appendix II:
Paula Danziger in London:
An Interview

Transcription of interview in London on National Public Radio's *All Things Considered*, 16 January 1993, Segment #9: U.S. Children's Author a Hit in London

KATIE DAVIS, HOST: For years American novelist Paula Danziger has had a big following among young people in this country. She's won their affection through a series of books with titles like *The Cat Ate My Gymsuit* and *Can You Sue Your Parents for Malpractice?* Danziger's books deal with the everyday plagues of early adolescence—parents, pimples, things like that. The books are all set in the U.S., but the issues are universal. And now Danziger has found success across the Atlantic in Britain. From London, Vera Frankl reports.

[Sounds of children at a playground]

VERA FRANKL, REPORTER: Lunch break at a school in a north London suburb. Hundreds of kids, socks down, hair flying, push and shove, kicking balls or each other across the playground. The literary inclinations of this little lot are not immediately obvious, but this day even those with little time for the written word are experiencing a rush of affection for the world of books. It's not hard to see why. Afternoon classes have been canceled because an author is coming to visit.

As the kids are rounded up, Paula Danziger arrives, coolly picking her way through the mayhem. Pixie-haired with spangly shoes and rainbow shirt, she appears to have raided a jewelers on her way to London. On her shoulder sits the pièce de résistance—a silver reptile brooch the size of the average iguana. Just looking at her is enough to make you sit up and listen, but Paula, a former teacher of the eighth and ninth grade, knows other ways of holding an audience captive.

PAULA DANZIGER, AMERICAN CHILDREN'S AUTHOR: Do you have anybody in your school who looks like an angel but is a really good liar? Do you know people like that? Okay.

Well, I had this one student who looked like he didn't do anything wrong, and I'd say to him—let me get my teacher voice— one day I said to him, "Harry"—because that was his name— "Harry, where's your homework?" He said he was walking to school near the yellow line in the middle of the road. He said he was walking down it, checking it one more time, because I was his favorite teacher and he wanted it to be perfect, when a truck driver with a very long fingernail came along, signaled, and took his homework.

FRANKL: For almost two hours, she talks and answers questions about herself, her books, and the process of writing. If she feels interest flagging, she simply launches into the famous ghastly jokes her readers relish.

MS. DANZIGER: What's red and green and goes 100 miles an hour? A frog in a blender. What's red, green—I told you. What's red, green, and brown and goes 100 miles an hour? Same frog a week later. What's green and hangs from trees? Giraffe snot.

FRANKL: This appearance is one of dozens that Danziger's made at schools and book shops throughout Britain since her first book was published here five years ago. It may be a shrewd way of gaining exposure, but it also allows Danziger to be around children and to make sure her books are on target. On this occasion, the kids offer all the reassurance she needs.

1ST CHILD: I thought it was really good.

FRANKL: What did you like about it?

1ST CHILD: Everything.

2ND CHILD: I liked all the disgusting parts.

FRANKL: Naturally.

3RD CHILD: I think she's a nice lady.

4TH CHILD: Colorful, cheerful, and nice. A lot of adults wouldn't be like that.

5TH CHILD: She's more childlike than grown-up-like.

FRANKL: Danziger's the rare kind of adult who hasn't lost touch. She doesn't much care if your bed is made or if you've washed behind your ears. She's always been a rebel herself, and in the battle between kids and the rest of the world, Danziger's firmly on the side of the kids.

MS. DANZIGER: I think it comes out of wanting to be an advocate and wanting to give voice to and to protect people who are at that stage. My childhood was fairly painful and was demeaning in a lot of ways. I was not nurtured in ways that I think kids should be. I have an empathy for anybody who has to go through stuff that's not always easy and who does it—survives it with a sense of feeling and a sense of humor and also not invulnerability. And because it's kids, there's just an extra sort of allegiance.

FRANKL: British children, as Danziger points out, are no different than American ones, and they've responded equally well to her simple message—adolescence stinks, but with a bit of humor you'll get through it. In Britain, Danziger's books are among the major success stories of recent years, even if she's a bit diffident about saying so herself.

MS. DANZIGER: I get a really good reception. I mean, I feel funny talking about that. It sounds a little bit snotty. "I'm a great person; listen to me." But, no, I think some people were appalled because I tell a lot of snot jokes. You know, it's not very British, these snot jokes. But there is that sense of play and humor here that's a little offbeat, and the books do very well in this country. It's very nice. I'm telling you, don't ever ask me to make you a cup of coffee or parallel park, but the books do well here.

FRANKL: Danziger's success hasn't stopped at books though.

[Television program theme music]

FRANKL: This is BBC TV's Saturday morning children's show *Going Live*, an eclectic mix of pop music, cartoons, and celebrity interviews for children. In a brief appearance on the program, Danziger so captivated its producers that she now has a regular slot that many British authors would kill for. For 10 minutes each month, she talks to an audience of up to nine million children about any books that take her fancy. One week she decided to make the classics she'd chosen more accessible by grouping them under the heading "Books You Thought Would Make You Puke but You End Up Loving."

MS. DANZIGER: My job is to say, "Here are some great books, look at them, go to the library, buy them, do whatever you want, always be reading." That's what I do. I feel—I guess it's a little like being a cheerleader for books, and that's fine. It's fun, and then you—somebody comes up and says, "Oh, I saw you on television." And it's sort of what I practiced my signature in third grade for. I actually like it a lot. How shallow.

FRANKL: Danziger now divides her time between her home in Woodstock and an apartment in London. Not content with having taken the British publishing world and kids' TV by storm, she's already on to her next book—*Thames Doesn't Rhyme with James*—the first to be set in Britain. Danziger acknowledges it isn't bad going for someone her father insisted wasn't college material, but she doesn't plan to ease up just yet.

MS. DANZIGER: I've done a lot, and I'm proud of that, and I feel very good about that. There's a lot more in me that I would like to learn and do and—you know, and get to another level of both learning about myself and doing certain things. But there is another part of me that does go, "Na, na, na, na, na," and the other part that goes, "Oh, get on with it."

FRANKL: For National Public Radio, this is Vera Frankl in London.

Selected Bibliography

Primary Works

Novels

Amber Brown Is Not a Crayon. New York: Putnam, 1994.
Can You Sue Your Parents for Malpractice? New York: Dell Publishing, 1979.
The Cat Ate My Gymsuit. New York: Dell Publishing, 1974.
The Divorce Express. New York: Dell Publishing, 1982.
Earth to Matthew. New York: Dell Publishing, 1991.
Everyone Else's Parents Said Yes. New York: Dell Publishing, 1989.
It's an Aardvark-Eat-Turtle World. New York: Dell Publishing, 1985.
Make Like a Tree and Leave. New York: Dell Publishing, 1990.
Not for a Billion Gazillion Dollars. New York: Dell Publishing, 1992.
The Pistachio Prescription. New York: Dell Publishing, 1978.
Remember Me to Harold Square. New York: Dell Publishing, 1987.
Thames Doesn't Rhyme with James. New York: Putnam, 1994.
There's a Bat in Bunk Five. New York: Dell Publishing, 1980.
This Place Has No Atmosphere. New York: Dell Publishing, 1986.
You Can't Eat Your Chicken Pox, Amber Brown. New York: Putnam, 1995.

Articles

"The Danziger Prescription." *ALAN Review*, Fall 1979, 7.
"Facets: Successful Authors Talk About Connections Between Teaching and Writing." *English Journal*, November 1984, 24–27 (co-author with several others).
"I Followed the Sweet Potato." *Voice of Youth Advocates*, June 1979, 8.
Why I Will Never Win the Newbery Medal." *Top of the News*, Fall 1979, 57–60 (article given as anonymously authored).

Other

Introduction to John Ciardi, *Someone Could Win a Polar Bear*. Honesdale, Pa.: Boyds Mill Press, 1993.

Secondary Works

Books and Parts of Books

Donelson, Kenneth L., and Alleen Pace Nilsen. *Literature for Today's Young Adults*. Glenview, Ill.: Scott Foresman, 1985.

R., Margot Becker. *Ann M. Martin*. New York: Scholastic, 1993.

Something About the Author Autobiography Series, vol. 36. Detroit: Gale Research Company, 1984.

Articles

Abso, Jenny. "Older and Wiser?" *Newsday*, 6 November 1988.

Beeby, Rosslyn. "Bad Jokes Fuel for Best-sellers." *Sunday Observer* (Australia), 19 June 1988.

Freeland, Dennis. "A Conversation with Paula Danziger." *Writing!*, November 1988, 20.

Freeland, Dennis. "Paula Danziger's Young Adult World." *Writer's Digest*, January 1990, 40.

Goldberg, Jane. "A Classroom Full of Character." *Star-Ledger* (Edison, N.J.), 24 May 1990.

Haffke, Carol. "A Writer's Childhood Helps Tell the Tale." *Gold Coast Bulletin*, 16 June 1988.

Hand, Lise. "Author Paula's Whirlwind Visit." *Sunday Independent* (Ireland), 15 October 1989.

Martin, Sandra. "Kids Love Danziger and Her Funny, Feeling Books." *Toronto Globe and Mail*, 2 February 1982.

Reed, J. D. "Packaging the Facts of Life." *Time*, 23 August 1982, 65.

Richardson, Jean. "The Danziger Blitz." *Publishers Weekly*, 19 July 1991, 37.

Sima, Judy. "Paula Danziger." *Educational Oasis*, January/February 1992.

Tatle, Suzan. "Author Writes for Real Kids" *Courier-News* (Bridgewater, N.J.), 21 January 1991.

White, Pam. "Teacher's Teen Memories Turn into Popular Books." *Richmond News Leader*, 29 October 1979.

Yourstone, Wayne. "Students Exercise Creativity: Writer Guides Imagination." *New Tribune* (Edison, N.J.), 18 May 1990.

Book Reviews

Amber Brown Is Not a Crayon
Booklist, 1 January 1994.
Bulletin of the Center for Children's Books, June 1994.
Children's Book Review Service, April 1994.
Kirkus Reviews, 1 March 1994.
Publishers Weekly, 21 February 1994, 254.
School Library Journal, May 1994.

Can You Sue Your Parents for Malpractice?
Booklist, 1 May 1979, 1361.
Bulletin of the Center for Children's Books, June 1979, 172.
English Journal, May 1980, 91.
Journal of Reading, February 1980, 473.
Junior Bookshelf, April 1987, 97.
Kirkus Reviews, 1 June 1979, 641.
Langton, Jane. *New York Times Book Review*, 17 June 1979, 25.
Reading Teacher, November 1979, 217.
School Library Journal, April 1979.

The Cat Ate My Gymsuit
Booklist, 1 November 1990.
Bulletin of the Center for Children's Books, January 1979, 76.
English Journal, October 1979, 102.
Geng, Veronica. *New York Times Book Review*, 5 January 1975, 8.
Journal of Reading, November 1978, 126.
Kirkus Reviews, 15 November 1974, 1206.
Nodelman, Perry. "How Typical Children Read Typical Books."
   Children's Literature in Education, Winter 1981, 177–85.
Publishers Weekly, 7 October 1974, 62.
School Librarian, February 1987, 58.
School Library Journal, 15 November 1975, 1206.

The Divorce Express
Booklist, 15 September 1982, 112.
Bulletin of the Center for Children's Books, September 1982, 6.
Childhood Education, March 1983, 277.
Edelman, Diane Gersoni. *New York Times Book Review*, 13 February
   1983, 30.
Growing Point, September 1986, 4674.
Horn Book, October 1982, 516.
Journal of Reading, May 1983, 741.
Kirkus Reviews, 1 September 1982, 1000.

Ms., November 1983, 76.
Reading Teacher, October 1983, 65.
School Library Journal, October 1982, 158.
Voice of Youth Advocates, April 1983, 36.
Wilson Library Bulletin, January 1983, 419.

Earth to Matthew
Booklist, 15 September 1991.
Bulletin of the Center for Children's Books, September 1991.
Kirkus Reviews, 15 September 1991.
Publishers Weekly, 9 August 1991, 58.
School Library Journal, October 1991, 122.

Everyone Else's Parents Said Yes
American Bookseller, February 1990.
Booklist, 1 October 1989, 347.
Bulletin of the Center for Children's Books, February 1990, 134.
Kirkus Reviews, 1 October 1989.
Publishers Weekly, 8 September 1989.
School Library Journal, September 1989, 249.
Wilson Library Bulletin, May 1990, 84.

It's an Aardvark-Eat-Turtle World
Bulletin of the Center for Children's Books, June 1985, 183.
Interracial Books for Children Bulletin, Vol. 16, No. 8, 1985, 18.
School Library Journal, April 1985, 96.
Tyler, Anne. *Washington Post*, 12 May 1985.
Voice of Youth Advocates, June 1985, 129.

Make Like a Tree and Leave
Booklist, 1 August 1990.
Kirkus Reviews, 15 July 1990.
Publishers Weekly, 29 June 1990, 102.
School Library Journal, October 1990, 114.
Wilson Library Bulletin, March 1991, 810.

Not for a Billion Gazillion Dollars
Booklist, 1 September 1992, 56.
Publishers Weekly, 27 July 1992, 63.
School Library Journal, September 1992, 250.

The Pistachio Prescription
Allen, Jan B. "How Do I Know Who I Am?" *ALAN Review*, Spring 1984, 14.
Booklist, 15 April 1978, 1347.
Bulletin of the Center for Children's Books, May 1978, 140.
English Journal, September 1978, 90.
Journal of Reading, March 1979, 561.

Kirkus Reviews, 1 April 1978, 379.
Lanes, Selma G. *New York Times Book Review*, 18 March 1979, 26.
Publishers Weekly, 8 May 1978, 75.
Reading Teacher, October 1979, 48.
School Library Journal, May 1978, 75.

Remember Me to Harold Square
Bulletin of the Center for Children's Books, November 1987, 46.
Horn Book, January/February 1988, 63.
Kirkus Reviews, 1 September 1987, 1318.
New York Times Book Review, 13 March 1988, 35.
Publishers Weekly, 8 August 1987, 105.
School Library Journal, November 1987, 114.
Voice of Youth Advocates, December 1987, 233.

There's a Bat in Bunk Five
Babbitt, Natalie. *New York Times Book Review*, 23 November 1980, 36–37.
Booklist, 15 December 1980, 571.
Bulletin of the Center for Children's Books, December 1980, 68.
English Journal, September 1981, 76.
Kirkus Reviews, 1 January 1981, 12.
Los Angeles Times Book Review, 25 July 1982, 9.
Reading Teacher, October 1981, 71.
School Library Journal, January 1981, 68.
Top of the News, Fall 1981, 71.
Voice of Youth Advocates, April 1981, 34.
Wilson Library Bulletin, December 1980, 292.

This Place Has No Atmosphere
Bulletin of the Center for Children's Books, January 1987, 85.
Fantasy Review, June 1987, 42.
Horn Book, March/April 1987, 208.
Kirkus Reviews, 1 September 1986, 1368.
Publishers Weekly, 31 October 1986, 70.
School Library Journal, November 1986, 100.
Voice of Youth Advocates, February 1987, 283.
Wilson Library Bulletin, February 1987, 48.

Index

The Author

Kathleen Krull is a former children's book editor; as Senior Editor at Harcourt Brace, she edited novels by Patricia Hermes, Judy Delton, Lael Littke, and Anne Lindbergh. Currently she is a full-time writer, with recent books including *Lives of the Musicians: Good Times, Bad Times (and What the Neighbors Thought)* (Harcourt), a 1993 *Boston Globe/Horn Book* Honor Book in Nonfiction; *Gonna Sing My Head Off: American Folk Songs for Children* (Knopf), a 1992 ALA Notable Book; *Lives of the Writers: Comedies, Tragedies (and What the Neighbors Thought)* (Harcourt); the World of My Own series (Dutton); and two chapter books: *Alex Fitzgerald, TV Star* and *Alex Fitzgerald's Cure for Nightmares* (Little, Brown). She is the regular book reviewer for *L.A. Parent Magazine,* has a monthly column in the *Los Angeles Times Book Review*, and has written articles and reviews for the *New York Times Book Review*, *Publishers Weekly*, the *Chicago Tribune*, and *Kirkus Reviews*. She lives with her husband in San Diego, California.

The Editor

Patricia J. Campbell is an author and critic specializing in books for young adults. She has taught adolescent literature at the University of California, Los Angeles, and she is the former Assistant Coordinator of Young Adult Services for the Los Angeles Public Library. Her literary criticism has been published in the *New York Times Book Review* and many other journals. From 1978 to 1988 her column "The YA Perplex," a monthly review of young adult books, appeared in the *Wilson Library Bulletin*. She now writes a review column on the independent press for that magazine, and a column on controversial issues in adolescent literature for *Horn Book* magazine. Campbell is the author of five books, among them *Presenting Robert Cormier*, the first volume in the Twayne Young Adult Author Series. In 1989 she was the recipient of the American Library Association Grolier Award for distinguished achievement with young people and books. A native of Los Angeles, Campbell now lives on an avocado ranch near San Diego, where she and her husband, David Shore, write and publish books on overseas motor-home travel.